The
Comparison
Trap

Claire Dunbar

This book is dedicated to my husband Andy, my beautiful children Jacob and Amber, and to all of my family and friends.

The most important things in the whole wide world.

I love you all.

Claire xxx

"Comparison is the thief of joy."
– Theodore Roosevelt.

"Be yourself; everyone else is already taken."
— Oscar Wilde.

"Don't compare your life to others. There's no comparison between the sun and the moon. They shine when it's their time."
– Cassey Ho.

Chapter 1

Emma

Emma curled up on her sofa at 8.30pm completely exhausted, the same way she did every night. The house was a mess, toys were everywhere and you couldn't even see the laundry bin for the never-ending pile of washing that was both in and around it. The kids' bedrooms were absolutely covered; a Barbie village had been semi-permanently set up in the twin 5-year old girls' room and it was almost impossible to walk into her 8-year old boy's room without standing on a Lego piece. Heaven-forbid if you attempted to dismantle any of that!

But as she scrolled through all the pristine Insta homes with everything perfectly placed, her body ached as she dreamt of having things differently. She admired the beautiful playrooms where all of the toys matched the room's décor and were being played with by immaculately dressed children or sitting neatly on its shelf where it belongs. There was not a trace of a trail of destruction anywhere.

She gave a well-practised flick up of the thumb. The next image displayed a cosy, calm, peaceful, yet expensive-looking living room. In the centre of the room was an eye-catching media wall with a giant TV displaying the opening credits of Dirty Dancing and a panoramic fireplace glowing away beautifully. Decoratively placed on the double glass coffee table was a single glass of bubbly with the reddest, sweetest looking strawberry on the side. Also sitting in the centre of the table was a small mound of perfectly placed treasures; at its base is a chunky black Tom Ford book with a smaller white Chanel book sitting on top of it, and at the peak of the mound was a little tray with a Jo Malone diffuser and candle set. *The candle's lit and she doesn't even have any company*! she thought, knowing that if she ever were lucky enough to own a Jo Malone candle it certainly would never, ever be lit unless there was very special company to both enjoy and witness it. If it ever even got lit at all.

And the sofa. *Oh, the sofa!* It was the sofa of a mother's unimaginable dreams! It was beautiful, modern, sleek and plain white, and if she owned it, it would be covered in grubby fingers the second it was placed into the house. It was adorned with a chunky knitted cream throw, and the cushions were karate-chopped to perfection giving the look of absolute comfort. But the main thing that she noticed about the post was that there was not a toy in sight. She glared around her own living room with a twang of repulsion at all of the toys that flanked the edges of the room. Dust had started to settle where she had only just dusted that afternoon – *Eugh*.

Flick. #bathtimefun. Bath bubble suds covered every part of a little toddler except for his face. He even had a crown of bubbles and a dollop on his little button nose. He was playing with a single, solitary little yellow duck as he was laughing at someone behind the camera. The joy in his eyes glimmered as he was surrounded by the most pristine bathroom. It had an LED illuminated dropped roof, and the highest of spec round LED mirrors, and *you've got to be kidding* - a TV flush with the wall at the end of the bath protected by a sheet of glass. The bathroom floor was spotless, not a droplet of water anywhere. The bath's waterfall tap was so shiny that a complete, undistorted image of the child was reflected back into the camera. The scene was nothing like Emma's own experience of her kids' bath time just a few hours before.

***

The girls had all of their favourite bath toys out ranging from mermaid Barbies (of course) to happy meal toys, and a variety of baby spoons, bowls and empty shampoo bottles to mix up their magical potions. The splashes of water cascaded from the bathtub just like their squeals of laughter. The girls were now of an age that she didn't need to keep her eye on them like a hawk, so she could potter about upstairs trying to tackle some of the never-ending mess. She picked up all the clothes from the floor and chucked them into the washing basket, along with some that would fit from the laundry basket and left it at the top of the stairs with the intention of taking it down and shoving it in the machine later. She used a small towel to try and dry up some of the water on the bathroom floor but wondered why she even bothered as another giggle and a splash landed just where she'd wiped it.

"Right girls, come on. Time to come out now, it's time for supper and bed," encouraged Emma.

"Oh mum, just one more potion?!" said Fern.

"PLEEEASSSSEEEEE mum, just one more?!" begged Luna with those big blue eyes of hers.

Emma jokingly rolled her eyes with a flick of a side smile towards the girls as she sighed "Ok, 2 more minutes girls, and that plug is getting pulled!"

As the girls climbed out of the bath and wrapped themselves up in their pink fluffy towels, Emma pulled out a matching set of pyjamas for them to put on. As their Friday night tradition, they climbed into Luna's top bunk to watch half an hour of TV before they went to sleep. Dan made up a little tray of their favourite goodies to graze on: Nutella toast, strawberries, popcorn and marshmallows. This half an hour window gave Emma the chance to quickly run round the high-traffic areas of the house with the hoover, to at least get the crumbs up and feel like it wasn't so messy before she could finally sit down. She went over the hallway, the kitchen and the living room, pushing the toys to the sides of the room with the hoover as she went, making a mental note to pick them up later.

Dan went upstairs to put the girls to bed as Emma went up to see Jasper with a plate of toast with butter and Jam. He was concentrating on his latest Lego build which he had been working on for most of the night. All of his Lego sprawled across his desk in little piles, organised by size and colour.

"Oh, what's this one then, Jasp?" she asked as she ruffled his Chestnut brown hair.

"I'm working on a car for the future. Not only can it drive on land, but it can fly in the sky and float in the water as well!" he exclaimed. "So, the next time we go on an adventure we can take it with us and get to go in the water and see all the fish, and then fly above and see how far we have walked!"

His imagination was amazing, and she was fascinated with him and his creation. He was always producing amazing inventions. Emma gave him a peck on the cheek.

"When you've finished your toast, you've got 10 more minutes then I want you to brush your teeth and get ready for bed please. It's almost bed time." Jasper smiled and nodded as he grabbed the toast and took a massive bite while he focused on sticking a blue light onto his flying water car.

Emma closed the door lightly and looked at her watch. She wanted to blitz the kitchen before she put Jasper to bed, so that she could finally relax for the evening. To her delight, Dan had already got started and was washing the dishes whilst listening to 90's songs on the radio. She sneaked up behind him and placed her hands on his waist. He got such a fright that he jumped back and stomped on her toe.

"Owwww," she shouted.

"Sssssh, you'll wake the girls!" laughed Dan as he scooped the bubbles onto her nose, reminding her of the little toddler in the picture from earlier.

"Oi you!" she giggled as she planted a big kiss on his lips and transferred the bubbles onto his.

Smiling at each other, they got to work, clearing away all the junk-mail and toys that had accumulated on the worktops over the day. In the 10 minutes before it was time to say goodnight to Jasper, they managed to clean the surfaces, put the clean dishes away, wipe down the sink and sweep the floor.

"Team work makes the dream work!" said Dan as he slapped her bum on her way out. She smiled a cheeky smile as she rolled her eyes at him pretending to cringe at his absolute cheesiness. But she secretly loved it.

She returned upstairs to Jasper who was ready and tucked up in bed waiting for his nightly chat with his mum. It was one of their favourite parts of the day. They lay in bed and the same questions were asked every night. "What was your favourite part of the day?" and "What didn't go so well today?"

She often thought of the meme she once saw that had a little poem all about kids growing up, and not realising that the last time was indeed, the last time; the last time they lifted their arms up to be carried, the last time they sneaked through to your bed in the middle of the night or the last time they held your hand walking down the street. So, she cherished this little one to one time they had, knowing that her son was growing up so fast and that one day he wouldn't need or even want his mum lying on his bed chatting to him before he went to sleep. Every time she thought about it, it broke her heart so she savoured every cuddle and hand-hold he was still rarely willing to give her. Afterwards she tried to close her eyes and store the memory away just in case it was the last time.

When she returned downstairs, Dan had prepared a bag of microwave popcorn and two glasses of their current favourite beverage, a blood-orange gin and lemonade. She loved the sweet little gestures he would do, showing that he cared and still enjoyed their time together even after spending 14 years together. He had laid her blanket out and made a space for her right next to him on the out-dated sofa. It was second-hand and it was all they could afford when they first bought the house when she was pregnant with Jasper. As comfortable as it was with its soft brown corduroy-effect fabric, she tried to make the most of how tired it looked with the help of soft, fluffy throws and some cushions. But as she picked up her phone and scrolled through the endless stream of designer candles, scandi-vibe play rooms and #livingroomgoals, it just didn't feel enough.

Dan glanced towards her as he sensed her frustration and matched it as he flicked between The Secret World of Crisps on Channel 4, and Inside Greggs: 24/7 on Channel 5.

"I miss having Sky, at least that way I could watch one and record the other," he moaned.

Not wanting him to feel he was missing out on anything, she tried to sound upbeat "You know, you could always watch one, and then catch the other on plus 1?".

"You're joking!" scoffed Dan, "What, and miss Gogglebox? Not an option!" The sarcasm poured out of him with a smirk. He absolutely hated reality TV but endured her guilty pleasure for her. Seeing into other people's houses was so exciting for her – getting to see how others lived, how they communicated with their family members, and how their houses were just so tidy all of the time! But Celebrity Gogglebox – that was on a whole other level! Those big white mansions with fancy sofas, huge open plan kitchen-dining-living rooms with chandeliers that are bigger than her dining room table. This was what dreams were made of for Emma!

They spent the rest of the night cuddled up watching council-TV and by 10.30pm she was struggling to keep her eyes open. She was exhausted from a week of work, running a house and looking after her family. And after a night of doom-scrolling at all the Insta-worthy families and the #housegoals, she honestly felt a little bit deflated.

In bed Dan cuddled into her and stroked her face for her to turn around and embrace him. But she was so tired from her busy day she just closed her eyes and fell asleep, safe in his warm, loving hug.

***

Whoever decided early morning Saturday clubs were a good idea obviously didn't have to work and run a family home themselves. A long-lie might have been a good option to have, just sometimes. But the kids' swimming lessons were at 9am every Saturday morning, for the Millars, there was no chance. The weekends were always full on. Even though money was tight and it was the only time to catch up with the housework and chores for the week, Emma and Dan always found ways to have fun without spending much. It didn't matter where they went or what they did as long as they were spending quality time together as a family.

As she set out the kids' clothes for the day, taking pride in their appearances as always, she got dressed and applied a little bit of effortless make up while the kids pulled their clothes on. Dan prepared a special breakfast of homemade pancakes with the choices of golden syrup, maple syrup, bananas, strawberries and blueberries. The kids loved their Special Saturday breakfast and it set them up for the busy day ahead.

After swimming lessons, the first item on the family's weekend agenda was to tackle the Big Shop. Now, I know what you are thinking. Doing the weekly shop with kids in tow is most people's idea of hell! But Dan was so good at making everything an adventure. The kids were each tasked with getting all of the ingredients for a meal with a budget of £5. He gave them each a basket and off they went, Dan and Emma strolling behind them, picking up cheaper meals to cover the rest of the week.

First back was Jasper who had picked up meal deal of two pizzas and a side of potato wedges for tea.

"Easy tea means easy shop...and easy make!" Jasper boasted. Dan and Emma laughed at his sense of efficiency.

Next came Luna proudly exclaiming that she is creating chicken fajitas for tea, showing off her basket containing a packet of reduced yellow sticker chicken thighs, tortilla wraps and a bag of mixed wonky peppers.

"Ay caramba!" cheered Dan as he swapped the basket for a kiss, pleased that she managed to create a good meal whilst also managing to save some money.

"You get those skills from your mum!" Dan declared as he lovingly squeezed Emma's cheek, pulled her towards him, and kissed her on the head.

Finally, Fern came bounding round the corner with her red curls bouncing and falling down in front of her green eyes and rosy cheeks. "Mummy, I'm going to make chicken korma just like you make us at school!" she shyly told. She was so chuffed with the bag of rice, chicken and cheap jar of korma sauce! The twinkle in her eye made Emma's heart leap and she wrapped her arms round her.

"Oh, I am so proud of you," as she planted a big kiss on her cheek. "I am proud of you all. Well done kids!" She then kissed Jasper and Luna on the foreheads too, with pride beaming out of her and almost spilling out of her eyes. Her heart was so full.

The family jumped in the car and headed home, singing along to their favourite radio channel as they went. As soon as they got into the house, Emma and Dan unloaded the shopping and started to put it away. The kids ran straight into the living room pulling the Lego and Barbies out from the edges of the room where they were hoover-shoved to last night. Laughter came screaming from the living room as Jasper's newly created car playfully crashed into Barbie town and the girls roared for him not to. As Emma prepared a mid-morning snack of fruit and crisps for the kids, Dan quickly made up a round of sandwiches and a packet of biscuits for lunch later and popped them into his backpack.

The Millars loved where their little house was. It was on the outskirts of the city, close to the local primary and high school, doctor surgery, shops and a park. Everything a family needs. But their favourite part was the forest which had a secret entry way across the road. After their snack and a little down time at home after their busy morning, they all put on their wellies, grabbed the backpack and set off through the broken fence and overgrown bushes to explore their favourite haunt. Emma took pictures of the kids as they gleefully stomped in muddy puddles, carefully clambered up the log piles and wondered in the nature and wildlife all around them. The girls filled their pockets with the treasures of their adventure: pretty sparkly stones, a rainbow of flowers, and beautiful crunchy leaves from the forests floor.

After an outdoor lunch and adventure in the forest, the family headed home to get cosied up and decided on an impromptu afternoon of crafts. The girls laid out all of the treasures from their trip across the dining table and carefully selected which leaves and stones would be glued to their pictures.

She felt so appreciative and grateful for her little family. It didn't take much for them to have fun. And with a little smile on her face, she went to upload her pictures of the day and clicked onto Instagram. But before she did, her eye caught an image of a mum and daughter with matching swimming costumes frolicking by a swimming pool somewhere sunny. The next post on her feed was a shopping trip buying the latest autumnal fashion #ultraminiuggs and #treatyourself drinking over-priced Starbucks drinks. Her smile soon faded with an overwhelming feeling her pictures were suddenly not good enough. That she was just not enough. She put her phone back into her pocket, sighed, and started the evening ritual of tea – bath – story – bed.

Chapter 2

Monday mornings always started the same way for the Millars. The alarm went off at 7.30am and for a blissful moment Emma hoped it was Sunday: the one day of the week where she had the chance of a long lie. As she started to rouse, not knowing what was going on, she began to become aware of the crescendo coming from her bedside cabinet.

"How you can't hear that, I'll never know!" he playfully shook her arm as he clambered over her to turn the alarm clock off.

"Eugh, it can't be Monday morning. Not already!" moaned Emma, as she struggled to open her eyes.

"You've got 5 minutes before you need to go in the shower" Dan shouted as he climbed out of the cosiness and comfort of their old bed and started the shower.

She rolled over, unplugged her phone from the charger and automatically opened her favourite social media app. A daily habit she's gotten into without even realising she's doing it. By the time it's her turn in the shower, she has scrolled though about 50 posts of people having #thebestweekendever, #newweeknewstart with their meal preps and healthy breakfast smoothies ready to go, and God knows how many beautiful, pristine, immaculate homes. Emma rolled out of bed feeling inadequate before the day had even started.

Just as it went every day, she had showered, dressed, and headed downstairs to make breakfast. The kids got themselves dressed, made their beds the best they could and opened their curtains. Although the beds were never made perfectly, she encouraged them to do it themselves so that they would learn to take pride in their surroundings as well as not expecting someone else to do everything for them.

The family had breakfast together every day before Dan went to work and Emma and the kids went to school. She enjoyed getting to chat to her family, and hearing about their plans for the week ahead. She loved knowing that their bellies were full as they set off to start their day. To her, the fact that the kids were happy before they went to school meant they had a better chance of having a good day, and much more likely that they would be able to concentrate and work hard in school. It gave her so much satisfaction. And it was something that she did not take for granted. She knew that sometimes mornings could be stressful for some families. But for the most part, the Millars knew what needed to be done each morning, and they got it done so that they could enjoy what time they had left in the morning before it was time to go.

Emma was thankful for the fortunate position she was in. She started her job in the local primary school the year Jasper started in Primary 1. As a dinner lady the pay wasn't great, but together with the income from Dan's job, it was enough to tide them over. Prior to having Jasper, Emma had started working in a call centre when she had left college. She started on a small wage but over the years had become one of the top customer service agents in the company and as a result gained a couple of promotions. The way she had of dealing with customers making them feel valued and understood, whilst withholding the company's good reputation during efficient calls had won her awards. Literal awards! She won a trophy at the Annual European Call Centre Awards down in London one year – who even knew that was a thing! She loved her job, and the recognition she received for it kept her striving to be the best.

Each Friday, she and some of her colleagues would go across the road to the pub when they finished work. They would congratulate themselves on their good week, share the stories of the awful customers they had the pleasure of dealing with, and unwind from the stresses of the week with a bottle of Pinot Grigio.

One eventful Friday night, where she decided that perhaps two bottles of wine were needed rather than just the one, she and her besties were screeching away to "Wannabe" by the Spice Girls on the karaoke. She was giving it all she could and having the time of her life, not caring about what anyone thought around her. She didn't even notice the handsome guy in a suit who could not take his eyes off of her. He'd been watching her all night, in awe of her confidence as she chatted and giggled with her friends. And now she was up on the stage, he was absolutely mesmerised.

After the song had finished, he brought her over a glass of fizz and said he couldn't believe his luck that the actual real Emma Bunton was in town, and he just had to buy her a glass of champagne. She laughed a proper belly laugh.

"Well, you're *half* right" she giggled. "I am Emma, but not *that* Emma!" and she accepted the glass and downed it in one.

"And here was me thinking I'd have to work a little bit harder to get your name and number!?" he joked. She noticed the cheeky smile and glint in his eye as he swept his hair back from his face into almost a mini-quiff. She felt the bravado oozing out of him and matched him with the raise of her eyebrow.

"Again, Mr Hotshot, you're only *half* right" and she strutted away, keeping her phone number to herself.

Every Friday thereafter Dan would come to the pub hoping to see her again. But she was too busy having fun with her friends to take him on. After several weeks of persistence, he came back stronger and stronger each week without even a dent to his confidence. She couldn't deny his good looks and the attraction between them, and finally she began to think that she might actually be able to fit a little date with him somewhere into her life. And with this thought, she finally let him have her phone number. Before she had even got home that night, he had text her saying he couldn't wait to take her out on a date, and if she would be available for breakfast in the morning.

That was 14 years ago. And every Saturday morning since, Emma and Dan have had breakfast together. But since, then they have grown, as did their family with a few miniature versions of themselves that join them. Saturday breakfasts have always been Dans area of expertise. He plans and prepares the meal, and she looks forward to it just as much as she did the very first time. Her bold, cheeky, handsome man. And he worshipped the ground she walked on now, just as much as he did back then.

Emma's intelligence, ambition and the general way she is with people would mean that she was more than capable of doing any job. But the increase in wages and working hours would be outweighed by the astronomical childcare fees she knew she was lucky not to have to pay. But more than the financial side of things, being a dinner lady meant that she shared all of the weekends, evenings, and school holidays with her kids. It also meant that she never missed a class assembly or a sports day. As much as she wished she didn't need to work she didn't actually mind her job. The girls were all so lovely, the days always went fast, and she enjoyed preparing healthy meals with the top 40 on in the background and serving all the kids with a smile.

Apart from the pay, the only other downside to the job was the management of the school. There was nothing wrong with them as such, they ran a good school. The behaviour of the children was impeccable. The standards were high and any form of unkindness between the children was simply not tolerated. The children respected themselves and their peers. They also respected the adults, and the manners they possessed were second to none. Every child thanked her as she plated up their lunch, and they helped clear away their dishes and stacked them neatly on the trolley when they had finished. The school was the most sought-after school for miles around, and if you weren't in the school's catchment area then it was highly unlikely that you'd be granted a place. She knew of several families who already had one child in the school, and their siblings had not been fortunate enough for a place.

There was nothing that she could put her finger on about the management. There was no incident that occurred, or specific instances that she could think of that would account for her feeling this way. But the only way she could describe it was the down-right arrogance that radiated from them. And it wasn't always this way, but recently she experienced the *I-am-better-than-you*-feeling every time she was in their company.

Just then as she was preparing the vegetables for today's meal, the headteacher and her cronies walked past, clicking their heels as they went and she found herself staring at them. The head teacher glanced over at her with a fierce scowl and she returned the smallest half-smile and looked down towards the carrots she was chopping. She couldn't even lift her head up to look any further, and then they were gone. She did not know what she had done, but she felt dreadful. One tiny second of her day where nothing even really happened, made her feel even smaller than the miniscule smile she gave back to them. And it took her the rest of her shift to shake off that awful feeling. Rather than feeling like the successful, award winning business women that she once was, with a husband who adored her and children who thought the world of her, in her own head, she felt like she was nothing. Not strong enough to have the respect she once had,

and not powerful enough to have the big fancy house
and flash holidays. Just. Not. Enough.

Chapter 3

Kali

Kali lined up her phone on her tripod and pressed record, showing off her flawless manicured nails under the perfectly delicate and flattering lighting. She used the edge of her nail to carefully peel off the sticker on the new luxury pamper box that had arrived in the post yesterday.

"Ok, wow, I was not expecting this!" she gushed as she unwrapped the tissue paper off of the La Mer gentle cleansing foam. "I have been *dying* to try this for years, ever since I first tried their infamous face cream!" She lifted the product to the camera for a closer view for her followers and elegantly placed it to the side as she reached for the next item.

"Oh, I think I know what this one is, I'd recognise that smell anywhere!" as she peeled of the paper and lifted it towards her nose for a little sniff whilst she unwrapped the Espa candle "Aw yes! The Soothing one is my absolute favourite!"

Next, she opened a beautiful small box, "I just love Charlotte Tilbury's iconic Pillow Talk lipstick, I mean, you can't ever go wrong with a nude lip. And this one is my absolute go-to!" she exclaimed as she applied it to her perfectly-plump lips.

One by one, she unwrapped each of the items with a little buzz as she did. She laid out the spread of luxury brands on her silk bedding pillow, taking the time to promote each of the items while filming for her page. She spent the next two hours editing the 30 minute video into a 90-second reel and uploaded it with the hashtags #blessed #gifted #ad.

She ticked "beauty box" off of her to-do list and then pulled on her Uggs. It was quite a long walk to the hairdressers, but she didn't mind. She was tracking her steps on her Apple Watch and needed to hit 10,000 per day minimum. Together with the dog walk this morning, which should be enough to cover it. It gave her such satisfaction when she achieved her goals for the day. If not, a few laps round the house and up and down the stairs would ensure that her rings were closed before bed time: something she found herself doing regularly just to achieve her goals.

As she arrived, she noticed the smell of the diffuser on the reception desk. "Oh Shona, it smells amazing in here!" air-kissing each cheek as she did.

"Thanks so much for coming in, Kali. I really appreciate it" said the owner of Blow and Glow. "The last time you done some content for us, we couldn't keep up with demand and ended up having to take on two new stylists!"

"Aw, you're so welcome, Shona. I love to help out other local business women" gushed Kali. "And anyway, my hair is needing it. It's looking a little bit flat these days."

"Not at all, look at the sheen on that!" as she picked up the hair and examined it in the light.

She settled down into the salon chair with a glass of prosecco and an individually wrapped chocolate as Shona started to work her magic. Photos were snapped and videos were shot throughout the process, making the most of the salon's lighting that made her hair look extra shiny.

After the toner was rinsed off, she gave the hair a wee trim and finished off with a bouncy blow dry. She enlisted Shona's help to take some final pictures and film some content of the finished result and the job was done. Literally. This visit to the hairdresser was a job for her. Not only was the treatment free, but payment for doing the job was monthly appointments at the hairdresser for the next 3 years, and bottles of the super-expensive shampoo, conditioners and heat protection sprays that are "essential for maintaining the look". It was a win-win situation for both Blow and Glow and Kali. In return for constantly good hair days, Blow and Glow would receive hundreds more followers and likes to their posts, and with it, more clients. With a simple reel entitled "To the Salon" with the infamous sound clip from Teen Titans, showing the process from start to finish complete with a before and after, the interactions came flooding in. People literally travelled hundreds of miles just to get the same hairstyle as Kali Munro.

She enjoyed her walk back home. Autumn was by far her favourite time of the year. And as much as she loved summer, there was just something a bit special about how autumn made her feel. She loved wrapping up warm in her favourite autumnal colours, and even in her comfies she looked effortlessly cool. Her ribbed beige Alo Yoga leggings were tucked into her Ultra Mini Ugg boots, and she wore a long baggy cashmere cardigan on top of a white crop top. The fresh air lightly tingled her cheeks as her blow dry bounced in the light breeze and she kicked the golden array of leaves that speckled the pavement.

As she strolled home, she spotted a cute new coffee shop in town with a sign promoting their seasonal limited edition Pumpkin Spiced latte. She stepped inside the on-trend white herringbone metro-tiled entrance way, examined the menu chalk board above the barista station and ordered the seasonal special – she just could not resist. She took a quick snap of herself sipping on the cute white paper cup with the shop's logo diagonally across it and a simple orange outline of a pumpkin and two autumnal leaves. The caption was simply "I Like You a Latte" and tagged the business. Within 20 minutes of posting, she received a DM from the business thanking her for promoting their business as they had received over 200 new followers as a result. Not that she even noticed, the message just joined the other hundred or so that were sitting waiting on her reply.

It was almost tea time when she arrived home, Hugo could not be more excited to see her as she opened the door. The wee white Pomeranian looked like a fluffy cloud as he spun round and round, yapping for his owner's attention. She scooped him up for a cuddle and shouted on Michael. With no reply, she checked her phone and seen that he had text to say he was still showing a client around a house just out of town but he'd be home as soon as he could. She kissed

Hugo on the head and grabbed his Burberry checked harness and clipped his matching lead on. "Come on wee one."

When they arrived at the park, it was busy as usual. Kids were playing on the swings and scrambling up climbing frames, dogs were being walked by families and couples strolling as they held hands and chatted about their days. She smiled as she watched Hugo prance about the park as though he was a prince with his nose held high and his paws looking as though they were barely touching the ground as they lightly flicked the pavement. Content with his walk around the park, Hugo led Kali back home up the hill towards their house. She thought about her day and the jobs she ticked off her list as she admired her nails and brushed them through her newly styled hair. Just one more job for the day, and my work is done. *Life is good* she thought, as she took a breath of the autumnal air and smiled to herself as she strolled.

"Guys, if you have been waiting for your sign to order your meals from Cuisine – then this is it! Watch me as I prepare this tasty and nutritional meal in less than 20 minutes." She tapped the box with her nails in a way the ASMR videos do and pulled out the packaged ingredients. "It has everything you need to make the meal, which means there is absolutely zero waste." She snapped a close up and fancy camera work panning out over all of the ingredients. She put herself back in the spotlight again. "Which also means that you are saving money by buying only the amounts of ingredients you need! The vegetables are already prepared, so there is no time spent washing and chopping. The hard work really is done for you!"

She then zoomed in on using her boiling water tap, adding the pasta and stock to the pot and putting the lid onto simmer. "While that's bubbling away, I'll just chuck in the diced chicken and veg to the hot pan, and gently heat that up" as she gives it a little stir. The shot changes to cooked chicken and vegetables. "Now that's almost done, I just need to add the cream cheese, pre prepared spices, and a spoonful of the pasta water." She drains the pasta and adds it to the pan with the rest of the ingredients and gives it a good mix. She tops it off with a generous handful of grated cheese. "Et voila! Cajun chicken pasta!" she exclaims as she dishes it up into her luxurious pasta bowls. "It really is that easy to make your family a delicious and healthy meal in no time at all! To order your box, click the link below and add the code "kali20" for 20% off of your first 3 months subscription!"

As though it was perfectly timed, Michael walked through the door and she embraced him as she always did. He adored how excited she was to see him every time as he scooped her up with a big cuddle and kissed her on the lips.

"Hey good lookin', whatcha been cookin'?!" Michael questioned with a double raise of his eyebrows.

"Oh, its Cajun Chicken Pasta for that new job I landed from Cuisine," she smiled. "Can you really smell it?"

"Yeah, it smells amazing! And it looks like you've been busy!" As he nodded towards all the recording equipment and ring lights highlighting the pots, pans, and utensils. He picked up the bowls and brought them over to the much-too big for just the two of them dining table and she followed closely behind them with two glasses of red wine. The glasses were her favourite, and although they looked expensive; they were actually just cheap ones from Ikea, but she loved them. She has had them ever since they were in their very first flat and has always felt sophisticated when drinking from them. They looked so fancy but were only just a couple of pounds each. Even though she has come along so far since then, they remind her of where she came from and helps keep her feet on the ground every time that she looks at them.

After tea, they loaded the dishwasher then topped up their glasses. She placed them on the coffee table and cuddled up to Michael as he flicked the TV on. It was a massive TV that sat centrally on the media wall, with the fireplace giving off just enough light to create a cosy ambience making the vast living room feel snug and comfortable. On either side of the TV was 3 evenly spaced alcoves filled with just enough perfectly placed ornaments and trinkets to keep it decorative yet minimal. Kali's vision of her perfect home was achieved and she adored what she had created.

She glanced down at her to do list:

    ✓   *Beauty Box.*
    ✓   *Blow and Glow.*

And ticked off her final job for the day.

✓ *Cuisine content.*

Creating content and promoting it on her page was not only giving her lots of freebies to look good, feel good and even eat good. It was also her full-time job which paid her hundreds, if not thousands of pounds, for just a few hours work. All of her hard work was certainly paying off. And she was so proud of the little life she had crafted for herself.

Chapter 4

Even when Kali didn't wash her hair, girls were still envious of her flowing, velvety chocolate locks. Kali was a plain Jane in high school and no one ever commented on her hair then, even though it was pretty much exactly the same as it was now. She always wore it in a side shade and long. Sometimes she'd wear it straight, sometimes she'd wave it. Not that anyone probably even noticed. But now she has over 800k followers, she is never short of a compliment or two hundred. But these compliments aren't only online. Even on the street she has admirers approach her telling her they love her hair, or asking where she got her coat, or what perfume she is wearing. She doesn't know what changed as she still looks very much the same as back then. Only now she has grown out of her acne and the braces have gone leaving perfectly straight pearly white teeth. But she is still the same hardworking girl she always was. Rather than writing essays and passing her exams she now works hard promoting brands and creating and maintaining her social media platforms. She still smashes every goal she sets her sights on. Failure isn't an option. If one way doesn't work, then she will find another that does.

But without knowing it, she gives off this glow that exudes from her every pore. The way she walks about and carries herself; confident but never cocky, strong but always kind, beautiful even when little effort has been put in. It's not even what she wears, even though her clothes are always fashionable, gorgeous, and usually expensive, it's how she wears them. She is the kind of woman that women want to be, and that men want to be with. Kali has it all. The looks. The personality. The money. The house. The cars. The clothes. The lifestyle. The life that almost a million followers want to have. At 24, that is some power for a young woman to have.

And despite all of the hard work she has put in, she knows just how lucky she is to have it all. None of her friends from school have anything close to what she has. Sure, some of them have done well for themselves. They have fairly decent jobs, have cars and some own their own little houses and flats. Some of them even have nice cars, driving about in flashy wee Audi's. But Kali and her boyfriend drive around in a Range Rover and a convertible Mercedes. Their house is in the nicest part of town, perched on top of the hill and the lights from the garden illuminate the house to make it look like it is on centre stage, and everyone else in town is their audience.

But Kali worked hard to achieve everything she has. She wasn't thrust into the limelight and just handed a platter with all of these amazing things on it. It all started when she and Michael had moved into their first rented flat together. It wasn't in the best part of town, and it was one of the worst on the street. Everything was grubby and dirty and the only furniture they could afford was second hand and all mismatched. She found great satisfaction in slowly cleaning the place up making it more "liveable." She documented the process with before and after pictures. She learned various hacks through trawling the internet and soon her limescale-covered taps were transformed with a 2p piece. Her black, burnt-encrusted oven door returned to transparent glass with the help of a trusty dishwasher tablet. And kids' stickers were removed from bookcases with the help of a 99p Scrubba Sponge and some mayonnaise.

She was so proud of her efforts and how clean the house was becoming, that she shared a short compilation video of some of her favourite cleaning hacks. Each clip had a before picture, a little action shot of the cleaning in progress, then a gleaming after picture. There was very little editing involved, just a little crop here and there and the video was posted on her private page. Lots of her friends liked the post and it gave her a little boost.

In between the rest of her usual posts of walking the dog, places she visited with friends, and plates of delicious looking food, she uploaded a few more cleaning posts and noticed that they were starting to drum up some interest. She gained new followers that she didn't know, and the questions began to trickle into her inbox. "How long did it take you to clean the over door?" And "Does the 2p hack really work, or did you use something else with it?". Every day she'd wake up to more followers, comments and questions.

When the flat was finally starting to feel clean, it just didn't look right. She then realised that something needed to be done about the décor and furniture.

Michael was working long hours in an estate agents, trying to get houses sold and make as much commission as possible. The only income she had coming in was her student loan, and after rent and shopping there wasn't very much left for anything else, never mind buying new furniture. She just had to make do with what they had. In between essays, lectures and exams she created a to-do list of home-improvements room-by-room. She had to set herself goals and targets prioritising what would give the biggest impact for the least amount of money. She decided to set up a colour scheme for the flat so that she could use the same materials throughout. She settled on a neutral monochrome pallet of greys, whites and black - which was all the rage at the time.

The first room on the list was the living room, she really wanted it to feel nice when they had people round. The sofas were black leather, and although not the nicest looking of sofas they were comfy (well-worn) and cheap. And there was not a lot she could do about them – they had to stay. She could, however, upcycle the furniture. After watching a few videos online, she found herself giving the nest of tables a light sanding, and then applied a layer of grey chalk paint. It wasn't too taxing, but it took her most of the night making sure they were perfect and giving them a quick second coat before she went to bed. After a full day of lectures and upcycling the tables, she felt pleased with herself as she headed up to bed. She was excited with the progress she was making and transformation in her flat that was slowly taking place.

When she got home from uni the next day, after she checked to see if the tables were still sticky with wet paint or if they were ready to be set up, she excitedly positioned them next to the sofa and staged them with a simple white Aldi candle. It looked brilliant, like a brand new set of tables! She was so proud of herself and took several pictures trying to get the best angle. She posted a side by side picture of the before and after entitled "upcycle project number 1, let the home improvements begin!" and the comments started to come in thick and fast!

"This looks ace!"

"No way is this the same nest of tables?!"

"Can't wait to see what you do next!"

Kali went to bed buzzing again, proud of her achievements that cost only a little bit of effort, and very little money. But the last comment was running around in your head. "Can't wait to see what you do next." It gave Kali an idea.

Instead of going to sleep at 10.30pm like she normally did, she sat on her bed and turned on her laptop and started creating herself a new Instagram profile.

"DIYImprovements" she thought. *Nah, not personal enough.*

"KaliMunros upcycling adventure" *Nah, too long. And way too geeky!*

"MakingMyFlatAHome" *again, too long. And not specific enough.*

"athomewithKali" *there! that's it. That's the one!*

Within minutes, the account was created and set to public. She uploaded the same picture of the nest of tables that she had on her regular account, added some hashtags and posted the picture. It looked good, and it was a start. But it was so empty and just needed a little more. She then took the cleaning reels she had already created, applied a simple filter to them to adjust the lighting and make them a bit brighter, and added a variety of music to each clip. She uploaded the content along with as many hashtags that related to them as she could think of. Half an hour later, the page was started, with 10 posts and she was able to fall asleep with a smile on her face that only a proud sense of achievement can create.

In the morning, Kali woke up to 200 hundred followers on her new page. *Wow* she thought *that was quick!* She checked her diary for the day, wondering what she could squeeze in for her next home improvement and upload to her new page. She wrote down "upcycle TV unit." She jumped in the shower, taking care to tie her hair up so it didn't get wet. After a quick wash and minimal make up, she got dressed and Michael dropped her off at uni on his way to work. He kissed her on the cheek as she set off for her first lecture at 9am.

Business management was the only way she was ever going to go. She had known from an early age that she wanted to be her own boss. She could have so easily set up a business straight from school which would have no doubt been successful. But with 8 Highers and a soaring ambition to succeed, she and her parents decided that holding off for a few years and getting a degree would do her no harm. For her, it was just another goal to smash, and for her parents it was something she could always fall back on.

As always, she worked hard and passed her assessments and exams with flying colours. 2 years down, 1 to go, and the only way was up. She was learning how to run and organise a business, about marketing strategies and the operations of supply and demand. She loved fashion and had planned to set up a clothing boutique in town, and dreamed of being so successful that she would own a chain of boutiques up and down the country. She'd eventually hire ambitious staff to run the stores and she could oversee the vision and aims and make the big decisions. She knew if she worked hard, she could achieve her dream and nothing would stop her.

When she got home that day after uni, she could not wait to tackle the TV unit and tick another thing off her home improvements list. She had gained another 100 followers throughout the day and a boost to her confidence. Michael helped her lift the TV off of the unit. Although it wasn't particularly big, it was old and heavy and they did not have enough money to replace it if it was dropped. She gave it a light sanding and set to work straight away.

Before the end of the evening the TV unit was matching the nest of tables and was waiting to dry before it too could be proudly staged. Whilst she was impatiently waiting, she posted a story with the before picture saying, "upcycle pending – check back to see the finished result."

By the following night, Kali had over 500 followers, more than she had on her regular page. She had no idea how or why her page had grown so quickly, the followers just seemed to come out of nowhere. She and Michael positioned the unit and lifted the TV back onto its place. Now the pine coloured, faded unit was a cool shade of modern grey. "It's amazing what a lick of paint, new drawer handles, and a little bit of effort can do!" posted Kali. The comments soon came in thick and fast. And as proud as she was, the room just did not seem finished.

Over the following days she freshened up the walls with a fresh coat of paint and set herself a budget of £20 for finishing-touches. She enjoyed a challenge. After a weekend of scouring online market places, car boot sales and charity shops, she found a black set of IKEA candelabras that she'd had her eye on for a while, a purple vase (which she painted the inside with the leftover paint from the walls and posted an upcycle video with of course) and a pair of voile curtains from the charity shop all for a tenner. And then she used the last £10 in Home Bargains for a couple of cushions and a new throw for the sofa.

With the addition of the finishing touches, she created a video complete with background music with the caption "Room 1: living room. Transformation complete." Again, the comments rolled in and she found herself excitedly replying to all of her messages, this time struggling to keep up. She couldn't believe that so many people would be interested in a page filled with pictures and videos of her cleaning and decorating her tiny little flat.

After a couple of months and a couple of thousand followers later, she had started to receive gifts where companies wanted her to promote an item for them. The first was from Scrubba Sponge. They had been impressed with the sticker-removing hack and her growing following and wanted her to post other uses for the sponge. Along with a box full of sponges and cloths, they also sent her £100 for the pleasure of doing so. She. Was. In. Shock. She loved her little page and her following, replying to her followers and sharing tips. But now she was actually getting paid to do it. *Like, what?!!* It blew her mind.

As Kali's following grew, so did her fortune, in terms of both luck and finances. An online sofa company messaged her asking her if she'd like to try out a new sofa and asked her to choose one that she liked off of their page. In dubious disbelief, she spent time measuring the room and selecting which sofa looked the comfiest whilst matching the vibe she wanted to create. She didn't actually think it would happen. But here she and Michael was, a mere two weeks later, standing staring mouths ajar at the delivery of boxes that were taking over their whole living room.

To get rid of the old sofa quickly, and do a good deed, she posted a picture of it on an online marketplace "free to a good home." Although it had seen better days, it was so comfy and she knew that it would do someone else a turn whilst they too were starting out.

Instantly she received 7 messages of people asking to collect the sofa, but she clicked on the first one she received and said if she could come now and get it – it was hers. Within the hour a girl and her dad arrived with his van to collect the sofa.

"Oh, my goodness, thank you so much. You have no idea how much this will help me!" beamed the girl to Kali.

"You are so welcome" We got a new one and thought there was still plenty life in the old girl yet!" laughed Kali as she playfully patted the arm of the sofa.

"I have loved watching your transformations and cleaning tips, and I just couldn't believe my luck when athomewithkali's sofa popped up on my page. FOR FREE!"

"Oh" replied Kali, taken back, and a little embarrassed "you follow my page?"

"Of course, all my friends do! We love what you are doing with the place, you're such an inspiration to us!" she gushed as she looked around the cosy little living room. "I phoned my dad straight away and asked if he could come and pick me up to get it before someone else snapped it up!"

Michael helped the girl's father down the stairs with the sofa whilst Kali and the girl trailed behind chatting. When they left, she and Michael returned back upstairs, they unboxed the sofa, clipped it together and flopped on top. They melted into the sofa as it enveloped their bodies, feeling like it was hugging them tight. And at that moment, they both looked at each other and started to laugh hysterically. The kind of laugh that you just can't stop. Every time they took a breath and thought about what just happened, they started all over again.

They just could not believe the night they'd had. Someone actually recognised the sofa and knew that it was her sofa. An "athomewithkali" sofa. *Like, what?!* A girl she had never seen before, had never spoken to, knew no one that she knew or anything about her, but she actually recognised the sofa from her page. It just blew her mind! *Is this how it feels to be famous?* she thought.

And not only was she now being recognised, but she also got sent a brand new, absolutely beautiful sofa. An expensive sofa that a girl in a wee flat could only dream about in her final year of university, for free. Things like this just don't happen to regular people. And yet here she was. normal, plain Jane Kali with a brand new, expensive, gorgeous, free sofa. Since she set up her page she'd received sponges, cleaning products, candles and even a new blanket. But a sofa?! This just raised the game to a whole other level. And with her Business Management head, she soon realised that perhaps her dream boutique wasn't the only way to be a successful business woman. Perhaps, she should invest more time in promoting her page. And the rest, as they say, is history.

Chapter 5

Nicola

Nicola ran her home like she ran her school: in complete control. Everything ran like clockwork. There was a tight schedule and everyone stuck to it without a question of a doubt. If you didn't know any better, you'd think that it was her who was in the RAF and not her husband. But no one could blame James for rubbing off on her - he was hardly there. He spent most of his time on the base a few hours away, and only came home at weekends. Sometimes, he would be on detachment and gone for 6 months at a time. And as much as she loved him, she did not need him. She could manage very well on her own, thank you very much.

She was the kind of women whom it was impossible to guess her age. If someone told you she was 30, you would believe them. There wasn't a single wrinkle on her face, no crow's feet by her eyes or laughter lines. Her hair was sleek and shiny without a grey hair in sight. If someone told you she was 45, you would believe them. She dressed in power suits that weren't trending in the latest fashion, yet always looked immaculate and perfectly dressed. She carried herself with an air of sternness and determination that only someone with life experience could.

Although it was the start of the new school year, she fell into their usual termly routine immediately. As Head Teacher, she liked to make sure that she was in school every morning by 7.30am. The boys were left with a list of chores and things to be done before they left for breakfast club at 8am. They had to make their beds (make them, not just pull the covers up as they had tried once before. Only once mind, they wouldn't make that mistake again), open their curtains, have a wash and brush their teeth, pack their bags making sure they had their water bottles and all the jotters and equipment they'd need for the day. They had to leave the house exactly the way they found it. The rule in the Smythe's house was if you use it, you put it back. Anything that wasn't put back was put in the bin, and Nicholas and Jamie knew only too well how that rule worked.

Each evening the boys attended afterschool club until 6pm. During this time, the boys were expected to complete their homework. There were desks and computers available, and plenty of staff to help if they needed it. Lots of future teachers worked at the afterschool club to gain experience and top up their income whilst they were studying, so it was the perfect place to complete their work and give them the rest of the night for their clubs and any free time they might have.

Just before the afterschool club doors were closed each night, Nicola would collect her sons and take them home for dinner. She'd then spend the rest of the evenings ferrying them between their various extra-curricular activities. With only a year between them and similar interests and hobbies, she was lucky that they attended the clubs together. Otherwise, she would have multiple clubs each night and zero time for anything else. Now that the boys are 12 and 13, she drops them off for a couple of hours and uses the time to do the weekly shop, or put on a load of washing, or batch cook and meal prep for a few days in advance. She worked hard to utilise every spare second that was available to her.

On a Monday night the boys had swimming lessons, on Wednesday nights they had Scouts, and Tuesdays and Thursdays they had Kickboxing. By Friday night the boys were exhausted and had free time to socialise with their friends. But nowadays, that meant talking to their friends via a headset on their PS5. And that suited her just fine. The boys were enjoying themselves, and she could catch up on the housework so that the house was spotless for the weekend ahead.

On a Friday night James returned from base and caught up on the things he liked to keep on top of. He'd cut the grass, clean the cars, and always made time for a round of golf and a few pints on a Saturday afternoon. Nicola used that time for the things she didn't get to do mid-week. Saturdays she spent at the city's exclusive health club. She'd usually start with a swim, a few gentle exercises in the gym, followed by a spa and sauna. In the afternoons she'd have a beauty treatment which she had on a weekly rotation. Week 1: waxing. Week 2: hair. Week 3: nails, and week 4: lashes and brows. And then the cycle would start over again. This meant that she was always preened, pampered and looking her best.

Tea on Saturdays was always a take-away. She liked to make sure she had the most of her Saturday me-time it was the only day of the week she didn't work. Sundays for the Smythe's were family days. Between her, her parents and her siblings, they would each take it in turn to host. After a full day of family socialising with grandparents, aunties and uncles, cousins and siblings, she would spend every Sunday evening in the study working, planning for the week at work ahead.

Her time at school was managed just as tightly as it was at home. Between breakfast club and afterschool club, she had 12.5 hours to work per day. Most people think that if you work in a school, you only work 9am – 3pm. She used to laugh at that comment, but now it just grates on her. If she only worked 9-3, then the school simply couldn't run.

Most of her staff arrive at school around 8am, but she likes to make sure she has a head start on her emails and sends out any plans or communications for her teachers to read on their arrival. This gives her between 8-9am to attempt to make a start to her never-ending to-do list. From the time the children arrived until the time they left, there were always problems to resolve, solutions to find and behaviours to keep in check.

People have rights, but in this day and age, Nicola feels that people often forget that with their rights, come responsibilities. And by teaching this from a young age, she believes that you can instil a routine and structure on which society can grow and depend. From starting school as young as 4 years old, children are taught to line up like little soldiers and walk through the school without so much as a whisper. If anyone is caught talking, they turn around and march back to where they started and try it again. When adults are walking towards a door that the class is filtering through, the child must stop and let the adult pass before the rest of the line can continue. The children greet each other and adults with a "good morning" or a "good afternoon" as they pass each other. The children say please and thank you whenever it is necessary.

Nicola prides herself on the results of action and consequence. She believes, and as her research and evidence confirms, that every action had a consequence. If you are late, you are wasting someone else's time, and thus, your time too shall be wasted. If you are rude to someone, then any privileges you may have earned will be revoked. Manner's cost nothing but ignorance with cost you everything. A missed playtime. A set of lines to be completed in your own time. Copying words from a dictionary. And it worked. Rarely did any of these things actually have to take place, the rumour of the consequences was enough to keep the children of Mrs Smythe's school in check. Everyone was doing what they should be doing when they should be doing it.

Everyone wanted to impress Nicola. Her staff would do anything she asked and were always trying to pre-empt what she wanted to get her to like them. Eager to please, they would reply to the 9pm emails, sending reports before they were due and working way more than their contracted working hours covered. She is a great leader in most senses of the word. She made you work hard, but she always had your back and supported you. If you wanted to climb the career ladder, she would make sure you went on the right courses and gained the relevant experiences to make it happen. She was a good woman to have on your side. She called the shots, and her Senior Leadership Team made sure that they were carried through.

Whenever she walked through the school, the SLT followed just behind her with a notepad and pen awaiting any instruction that might come their way. Together, their presence sent a message to everyone: we are strong, we are powerful and we work together. Although everyone wanted to please her, the reason wasn't only just because they admired her, or even because they liked her. It was because they didn't want to disappoint her. And that was exactly the way that she wanted things to be.

Chapter 6

Fridays were always busy days in work. Nicola held a meeting with her SLT to ensure that all of the weekly priorities were completed, and that the next weeks priorities were set. She ran through her expectations and gave a list of jobs for Jackie and Donna to complete. They scribbled down their action points and made sure not to forget anything.

Just before the meeting ended, she received a phone call from her son's school. Normally she wouldn't answer a call during a meeting. In fact, it was rare for her phone to ring during working hours. However, she seen it was from her son's school and decided to take it. They called to let her know that Jamie did not hand in his homework, and when questioned about it, verbally assaulted his teacher and stormed out of the room, kicking the furniture as he went. Since it is not the first occasion where he has taken his anger out towards his peers and teachers, the school felt they should contact his parents to let them know about this gradual change in his behaviour.

"Gradual change in his behaviour?! Jamie is a top set student! Never would he act in such a way. Are you sure you have the right child?" she accused as her voice grew louder and her face redder. Embarrassed by voicing too much, she stepped out of the room for some privacy. The SLT followed her out into the corridor to make sure everything was ok and if there was anything they could do.

"Get back in there!" she snarled at them, shaking her head in anger as they sheepishly sulked back into the conference room.

The high school confirmed her worst fears that it was indeed her youngest son who was showing her up like this. She just couldn't understand it. Jamie had always just done what he was told. He had his mum giving him perfectly clear instructions, and his big brother Nicholas to ensure that he carried them through. He knew right from wrong from a very young age, and he knew better than to cause any bother for his mother.

She grabbed her belongings from the desk and marched through the school with the two of her SLT's flanking her, petrified that they had upset her. She thrust open doors, clip clopped loudly down the stairs and marched through the dinner hall to get back to her office. She caught the eye of one of the dinner ladies without even being aware of her and looked right through her as she stomped. It seemed as though she had forgotten her own manners that day.

She could hardly concentrate on her job and list of things to do and people to deal with. As soon as the bell went at 3.15pm, she drove straight to the high school to pick up the boys and take them home. *No afterschool club tonight* she thought, she just had to get to the bottom of this and sorted out what really happened.

As soon as she saw the boys, she knew from Jamie's face straight away that things were as bad as she feared. He could feel her anger as he walked towards the car and couldn't even lift his eyes to look at her. The fury started to bubble up inside her like it hadn't for a long time. The boys got in the car and she drove all the way home without anyone saying a word. When they arrived, she unlocked the door and walked through to the dining room table throwing her keys down a little harder than she had liked. She pulled out her chair and went to sit down as she heard Jamie kick off his shoes and start to walk up the stairs.

"Don't you dare. You get here and explain to me what is going on!" she demanded.

Jamie paused on the stairs as his mum shouted at him then he lifted his foot and continued up into his bedroom.

How dare he ignore me?! she raged as she stormed up the stairs into his room.

"What on earth has gotten into you, Jamie?" she pleaded.

He just lay on his bed staring at his feet.

"Jamie, you know better than to ignore me! What is happening to you?!" she challenged.

"You really have no idea, do you mum?" he spoke as he looked into his mother's eyes with a hurt she hadn't seen since he fell and grazed his knees when he was about 3 years old. This wounded her. This was not the reaction she anticipated as the anger bubbling inside her seemed to dissolve as it caught her throat. She just looked at him.

"What do you mean?"

"What is the point mum? In any of this? We don't have fun. We never do anything. We just complete chores and do what you want us to do."

She couldn't believe what was coming out of her son's mouth. "What are you on about, everything I do is for you? Look at everything you have, look at all you do. You have EVERYTHING!" The anger returned and the tears that had threatened started to dry up.

"All of this cost's money you know! None of this is for free! YOU DON'T KNOW HOW LUCKY YOU ARE!"

Jamie matched his mother's emotions and sat up, his face scrunching up to challenge her but before he could even speak, she marched over to the play station and pulled out the controllers from the console.

"Your actions have consequences, Jamie!" she screamed as she slammed the door. Jamie's night of socialising with his friends went out the door along with his controller.

Normally she didn't have to raise her voice. Her reputation proceeded her and people generally just done what she wanted them to do. How she reacted tonight was very unlike her, and she didn't like it. She had lost control of the situation and acted in a way that was way below her high standards. She knew better than to raise her voice at a child and allow her emotions to take over. But what you put out into the world; you get back. Every action has a consequence.

Frustrated at Jamie, but also at herself, she marched downstairs in an overwhelming emotional state. She walked over to the table, her feet feeling like lead, and picked up her keys. She ran her fingers over the dent in the soft wood she had just created. She realised that the damage had already been done and the tears that had been threatening to flow all day finally made their way out of her eyes. She placed her elbows on to the table sobbed into her hands for the first time in a long time.

Nicholas stood in the background watching his strict, intimidating mum cry like a baby. He did not know whether to give her the space that he thought she needed or to go over and put his arms around her. He hesitated. Normally it was her who would lead the way and tell him how to deal with any situation which arose. He thought of his options and decided on going upstairs to his bedroom. He felt helpless knowing his mother and brother were crying alone and didn't do anything to help either of them. He lay on his bed and turned his headphones up to maximum volume in an attempt to drown out his feelings.

With his father away, he was told to "be the man of the house" whilst he was gone. But this situation here showed Nicholas that he just wasn't as capable of doing so as he once thought he was. His little brother had effectively stepped on his toes by breaking the rules that were enforced by him and set by their mother. His position as big brother felt threatened. The once strong structured house felt weak and ruptured.

Normally it was his mum who fixed things. But this time, it was her who was broken.

Chapter 7

Emma

Emma finished work an hour before school ended which gave her a little time to herself to prepare tea before she had to pick the kids up, and she loved this little magic hour. A tiny, small slither of the day to give her some time with nothing but her own thoughts. She used it to her advantage to get a little step ahead of the game and do some chores and prepare the evening meal. Then it meant that she could enjoy a little more time with the kids before the weekly evening bedtime routine began. Sometimes to mix things up a bit she took them to the park to play, or to the library to choose and read some books together. Jasper was at an age now where he could amuse himself, and the girls had each other to bounce off of and keep each other company. She adored just watching them interact with each other and the world around them. Sometimes when she thought about it, she marvelled at how she was able to produce such beautiful, remarkable little human beings. It took her breath away at how much she loved them. All she wanted in life was for her family to be happy. To have the things that she never had growing up.

It wasn't that she didn't have a happy childhood. Her parents gave her the best they could with what they had. She always had food to eat, a warm bed to sleep in and a toy to play with. There weren't ever any holidays abroad, or even any staycations or camping. There weren't day trips to zoos or the cinema. The money just wasn't there, and neither was the time. Her father worked as a painter for a local firm and would work long days and every homer he could get at weekends just to help make ends meet. Her mother was a cleaner at the local hospice and worked every evening. There was no one to help with childcare, so the parents were rarely together and had to juggle raising children and working full time between themselves. Between parenting and running a house along with working every hour available meant there was hardly any time to be spent with their children. But more than that, there wasn't particularly any nurture. There were no cuddles for the sake of cuddles, there were no playful kisses on the forehead, there was no praise when you done something well. There was hardly any praise ever. There were just high expectations, and if you didn't meet those expectations, then expect to be punished for it. But Emma wasn't much different to her peers around her. That was how it was for her and her friends. Tough love. Get it done. Pick yourself up and get on with it.

Emma doesn't blame her parents for the way she was brought up - she knows that they have always loved the bones of her. That's just how it was back then. They didn't know any different. But they done everything they could for her. They went without for her. Not that she was aware of it at the time, but looking back she realised that sometimes her mum would skip meals just so that she and her siblings could have a meal. Her parents always wore the same few sets of clothes, so that when the kids had out-grown all the hand-me-downs they had, they could get new clothes. And birthdays and Christmases were always special. Her parents scrimped and saved so that there was a fancy meal, special candles and gifts to be opened.

Now her parents try every day to make up for it with their grandkids. They are always visiting and asking to take the kids away out for ice-cream and a walk to the park. Or shopping to get some new clothes or a toy now that they have a little more money and can afford to. She appreciates this so much, as money isn't often available for such treats from her and Dan. But more than the money that is spent, she loves how much time they spend with their grandkids and adores watching how her parents love her children. They treat them as grandparents often do - without the pressures and anxieties of trying to raise a good-human being that parents frequently feel. They have the experience of knowing that nothing lasts for ever and can just be kind to them, have fun with them, and let them off with a little more than Emma and Dan ever would have. They allow chocolate before bed, or another sweetie even though they have already had too many. Or sometimes even a wee sip of grannies Diet Coke knowing that their parents would never allow it. Emma loves watching the relationship between her parents and her children; the joy that emits from her parents faces as the girls sat on their knee giggling as they are tickled, or as Jasper shares a story about his latest Lego model or computer game. She knew that her parents would have done more for her if they could.

But that just made her all the more conscious of trying to do her best for her children, to get it right as best as she can. Although money was short, as well as making sure their physiological needs and safety needs were met, she also prioritised their needs of being loved and a sense of belonging were met too. She wanted them to develop their own self-esteem and realise their true potential in life. The world really was their oyster. And she would do everything within her power to raise human beings capable of fulfilling their wildest dreams.

All of these thoughts of creating the best lives for her children, brings her back to her own sense of fulfilment. She knew she wasn't achieving her full potential and she ached for having more. She wasn't greedy, she thought. All she wanted was a nicer wardrobe, a better car, some holidays in the sun.

But more than any of that, she wanted a house she could be proud of. It didn't need to be massive, just big enough like some of the beautiful houses she scrolled through on the gram. She dreamed of a house with a cosy living room she'd call "The Snug" even though there would be nothing snug about it. She dreamed of a huge sofa that felt as though it was hugging you the moment you sat down on it, a plush carpet that made you feel like you were walking on clouds, and a massive media wall complete with a cosy panoramic fireplace that you could see from all angles of the room, complete with an Odeon-worthy TV screen. There would be fancy ornaments and decorations that would be strategically placed throughout the room, but absolutely far from cluttered. Just enough to make you think wow. Everything would be clean, neat, and tidy. There wouldn't be shells and rocks picked up from every visit to the forest or the beach. There wouldn't be toys that covered the floor by day, and flanked the edges by night as the Dyson pushed it there to make it at least feel clean, if not tidy.

She fantasised about a sleek, white kitchen with gold handles and decorated with oak chopping boards, fancy candles and gold taps and accessories. A kitchen where there weren't appliances cluttering the worktops, only minimal but beautiful plants and an expensive coffee machine that would make any café envious. The bifold doors would open out into the garden which would really just be an extension of the house, with an outdoor dining table complete with a central firepit on top where they could toast marshmallows and keep themselves warm on a cool summer's night. She wished for the greenest stripy-lined grass, with a pergola topped hot tub on a gorgeous porcelain patio. She didn't even know what a porcelain patio was – she imagined a delicate China which could easily break and hoped it wouldn't be anything that resembled that, but all she knew was that it was trending and that it looked stunning. The hot tub would be edged by two all-weather sun loungers that would look just as gorgeous in the summer as they did in Autumn. Providing the perfect place to sip on a clear glass of iced coffee and read the latest book 'til her heart was content.

She yearned for a house where she could happily host her friends for a cosy movie night, with snack plates filled with fun Friday night treats. Or where she could invite her whole family round and enjoy each other's company and nibble on a grazing table filled with everything from pretzels, crackers and cheese, and pork pies, to strawberries, gourmet marshmallows and chocolate dipping sauce, all displayed on the table top like a carpet of delicious food, waiting to be nibbled on throughout the day.

She desired a house she could show off, a house that she would be keen to share pictures of with the world. Not the little box of toys and outdated, mismatched, second-hand furniture that she currently resided in.

Chapter 8

Nicola

The Smythe's family home life began to deteriorate ever since that Friday phone call. Jamie was becoming more and more defiant as each day went on, refusing to follow his mother's rules. It started off lightly at first, just little things that happen in every house-hold from time to time; his bed was left unmade, his towel was left on the bathroom floor, his clothes weren't put into the washing basket. She tried to keep calm, but she became so frustrated at his attitude and downright poor-choices that arguments occurred every morning and every evening.

As she liked to say, actions cause consequences: because his clothes weren't put into the washing basket, he therefore had no clean clothes to wear. She ended up getting so angry with him and to prevent any more fights he'd just pick up dirty clothes from the floor and put them on.

"See!! There's no problem now! No clothes on the floor! And I have clothes to wear!" he screamed back at her.

For someone with two degrees, and a Master's in Education, you would think that she would be aware that Jamie was reaching out to his mum the only way he knew how to get her attention. But because he wasn't doing the things he should be, the house was no longer running smoothly and she was punishing him for it. In doing so she shot him down and pushed him away even further. If this were any child in her school, she would know straight away that this dramatic change in his behaviour would be a cry for help. But she just could not see what was right in front of her.

It wasn't only Jamie that had changed. Nicholas had started to rebel too. Although he was never aggressive or argumentative towards his mother, he became withdrawn. If he saw that Jamie was getting away without doing any chores, then he would follow suit and do the same. He didn't find it fair that he should have to do all the work and Jamie gets away with doing nothing. So, he didn't either.

With the change in the boys also came a change in Nicola herself. She ended up coming into work later every day as a result of the stress and arguments and things not being done. This meant that she didn't have the time she needed to catch up on emails and send out notices and work to her staff. She would start school in a terrible mood and be unable to improve it over the course of the day. A job she once loved, she found she no longer had the passion for. People who once wanted to impress her now found themselves being made to feel inferior. She would criticise them for making mistakes, even though they weren't really mistakes, they are just things done slightly differently from how she would have done them. They were intimidated by the very person who should be leading them by example.

Just like her staff, she came home every night deflated. She knew she wasn't fulfilling her potential and that she was more than capable of doing a better job at work, and she hated being there. After a while, she soon began to dread coming home too; it was no longer the place of blissful routine that she worked hard to create. She found ways of staying at school longer to avoid going home; she made meetings last longer than they needed to, and organised additional training for staff that they so clearly-needed as they were "unable to follow simple procedures." A once sought after school became a toxic place with low morale. The teachers began to feel as if they were not good enough. People started taking more sick days because their mental health was being affected and they felt unable to cope with the pressures at work. Then, with a reduction in staff but the same amount of workload, more work was piled onto an already struggling staff and the work-place hit an all-time low.

Teachers, being the special type of people that they are, generally always want the best for the children. That's why they became teachers in the first place. God knows, it isn't for the working conditions or the money! They worked hard to make sure that the classrooms were the happiest place in the land as always, where learning was fun and interesting. Children still adored coming to the place they got to spend time with their friends and felt seen by their teacher. But maintaining this image was about all the staff could handle, and anything outside of that became almost impossible. Conversations in the staffroom at break and lunch became so strained that people soon avoided going – they stayed in their classrooms and worked instead of taking their breaks. There was no release for staff in an already stressful work environment. What once was weekly meetings with banter and fun thrown in for good-measure became a dumping ground where people aired their frustrations. And all of the unnecessary training only further added to their feelings of inadequacy and incompetence.

The tension could be felt from everyone, and, as children do, they began to notice the shift in the atmosphere. Behaviour started to become a concern in the playgrounds which then permeated to the classrooms. When teachers called for help, they were made to feel even further incapable of performing well in their jobs. Where they should have been supported, they were criticised. With the lack of a united front, the consequences were no longer consistent. Soon, there was more rudeness and impoliteness, and the behaviour of the children were impacted which resulted in more conflicts and fights.

This therefore meant the SLT were having to spend more time dealing with issues, and less time doing the job that they normally did. The school changed from being an efficient, supportive, positively-driven place to work. To a toxic, negative workplace where people no longer wanted to be. And it showed.

Chapter 9

Kali

Although Kali didn't have a regular 9-5 job and therefore no place to be by a set time most mornings, she still liked to get up early and make the most of each day. She set her alarm for 7am but generally woke up before then with the sound of Michael tip toeing out of the room to his bathroom for a shower. She rolled over, looked at the notifications on her phone: thousands of likes, hundreds of comments, and a list full of DMs. She put her phone down and smiled as she rolled over and pulled the cloud-like duvet over her head. She dozed for 5 more minutes, enjoying the peace before she started her day. Michael must have finished his shower early and jumped on the bed wrapping his arm and leg around her.

"Hey! I'm enjoying 5 minutes of peace and quiet here!" she giggled.

He pulled off the covers and gave her a big kiss and started both of their days off with a bang. Literally.

Although they both had extremely busy lives and successful careers, their number one priority was always each other. Whilst he got dressed, she wrapped herself in her silk dressing gown and went downstairs. She opened the fridge and put a slice of fresh lemon into a double walled glass mug and poured boiling hot water straight from her fancy tap. She then popped in a few ginger and lemon ice cubes from the freezer to cool it down enough to make it drinkable straight away. She sipped on it as she washed her favourite fruits and vegetables and popped them into a blender to make two smoothies. She placed her vitamins on a small plate next to her wooden-lidded glass tumbler filled with the purple smoothie and snapped a picture. She uploaded it onto her profile straight away #newweeknewstart. The hearts came before she even put her phone down.

The scent of Michael approached Kali before the sight of him did. He smelled strong, masculine and sexy. She turned round as he strolled into the kitchen dressed so charmingly in his navy Hugo Boss suit with the top button undone on his crisp white shirt. He was effortlessly handsome. Even with a little blonde stubble and rugged shower hair he looked immaculately fresh and clean. She walked to meet him with his smoothie and they sat at the breakfast bar and laughed and chatted about their plans for the day. He told her he'd made reservations at the local top-end expert steakhouse, and to be ready for 8pm. She loved how romantic he was. She checked her diary and mentally rearranged her day to fit in the new, last minute plans.

After Michael left with a kiss, she clicked the lock of the bifold doors with her thumb and slid them open to her garden. The porcelain tiles of the huge patio mirrored the floor tiles of the kitchen flawlessly. She went back over to the breakfast bar and swallowed her vitamins one-by-one, gulping them down with sips of her now lukewarm lemon ginger water. She picked up her smoothie with its glass straw and her book and strolled barefoot out to the outdoor table. She put down her things and pulled out her roll mat from the storage box. Although it was cold, the pergola limited the wind and a welcomed, gentle breeze swept past and lightly lifted individual strands of her hair.

She started off her routine with a Tadasana, standing with her hands pressed against her side and feet pressed together rooted to the floor, reminding herself to pull the crown of her head up to the sky. She could feel the muscles in her quads and tummy tighten and her breathing regulate as she held the pose. Although she has attended many a yoga class over the years, she has recently been enjoying taking the time for herself and being outside in the privacy of her own garden with nothing but the sound of the wind in the trees and the bird song.

After her usual 20 minute routine, she wiped the tiny beads of sweat from her face and sat on her all-weather comfy chair. She opened her book and sipped on her smoothie as she read the words of her favourite author. She loved starting her day this way. Carving this special time for herself meant that she felt energised yet grounded, ready for a productive day ahead.

In her diary for the day was create and post content on the vitamins (check), do a make-up tutorial using the new items that were posted to her last week, get her nails done and film some new home-content. She wanted to do a wee cleaning post, keeping in with her roots and her loyal followers. She just had to do a light case of dusting and placing down her bits and pieces. It's not much, but her followers seem to go mad for it. They also seem to love shots of the garden. Only last week she filmed herself sweeping up the leaves in the garden, and then lit the firepit and it had over 300,000 likes within the hour! But she didn't often need to clean. They had a cleaner to help keep on top of the house, with its massive rooms and multiple bedrooms and bathrooms. Although there was only the two of them and they were generally really tidy people, it just made things easier and gave her more time to create and film content and Michael could spend his time working his way up the career ladder.

Oh, and add Date Night to her diary she remembered. She picked up her fluffy pink pen to scribble it into her diary. She picked upon their latest trip to Florida, it had a Minnie mouse topper on a spring that bobbed about as she wrote. She smiled of the memories of their holiday and the fun-times she and Michael had together as she finished writing and placed the ribbon to keep her page. She shut her diary and returned it back to its drawer. She then took off her dressing gown and hung it up on its hook on the back of her bedroom door. Since the spontaneous date night was now happening, she upgraded today's shower from a body wash to full-blown procedure. She switched on the rainfall shower head which was reserved only for hair-washing days. She lathered up from head to toe, the luxurious scent filling the room and her nose as she set to work scrubbing and removing every trace of bodily hair.

She dried herself in circular motions with the whitest, softest, fluffiest towel. She applied her favourite face cream and serums, and her whole body with body lotion. She spritzed herself with Dior Addict, inhaling her favourite scent as her face beamed in anticipation for the date.

She pulled on a crisp white t-shirt and tucked it into her favourite blue jeans. They were hugging in all the right places, and oh-so-comfy with a wide leg. She threaded a black Gucci belt through the loops and paired it with a pair of black suede Birkenstock clogs. She set up the box of make-up and laid it all out on her dressing table. She set up her phone on the tripod and was ready to begin filming under the illumination of her ring light.

Kali took 45 minutes to apply her make up, explaining the whole process as she went. She always prided herself on working hard, but today she paid particular attention to the details to make herself look as effortlessly glamourous as she could. Her skin was dewy, contoured and highlighted in all the right places. Her eyes popped as she used subtle eye shadows and eyeliner on the waterline. She lined her lips in a slightly darker shade than the nude lip gloss she wore and made them look even plumper than they naturally were. When she was satisfied with the final look, she stopped recording and turned off the ring light, picked up her phone and laptop and headed downstairs. Whilst she waited on the content downloading from her phone to her laptop, she made herself a quick chicken salad. She used spices to coat the chicken and popped it on the grill. She opened her giant American

Fridge Freezer and chose spinach, peppers and spring onion from her very organised vegetable crisper drawer. She took the time to carefully chop the veg and layered the chicken on top with a sprinkle of vinegarette.

She worked through her lunch as she usually did, munching on her salad as she edited her make up tutorial. Once it was edited and uploaded to her social media platforms, she gave the kitchen a quick tidy. She wiped down all the surfaces and loaded the dishes into the dishwasher and all traces of lunch were gone. She snapped a quick before and after and decided to save these pictures for later on in the day. She couldn't possibly post two pieces of content so close together. She liked to tease her audience, give them enough to keep them interested, but just enough so that they always wanted more. Supply and demand; something she learned a lot about at business school.

Kali walked into her wardrobe and scanned the rows of clothes deciding which would go best with her outfit and finally settled on a cream blazer. She went to her bag section and scooped up the straps of her trusty Neverfull on her arm. After popping her phone and keys inside, she made her way downstairs to set off for her nail appointment. She has been going to the same salon ever since she started getting her nails done, way before her social media platform and influencer lifestyle took off. Carly always took the time to get her nails exactly the way Kali wanted them, and even when she asked what she wanted and her response was "surprise me," Carly seemed to know even more than Kali what she wanted. She loved the simple, classy look and Carly always just managed to nail exactly what she wanted: literally and figuratively.

At the start of her career when she had not long qualified and was working from a room at her parents' house, she was kind to Kali, and even now with her own successful nail salon she is still exactly the same. Treating her no different despite all the growth they have both gone through. And Kali liked that. She could trust her with anything and over the years they became close friends. As usual, they giggled and chatted throughout the appointment.

"So, what are you after today?" Carly asked as she scanned her nails. They were a simple modern French tip manicure. Her natural long almond nails were a nude with the slightest tinge of pink, with only the top 2mm a curved stipe of white. A classic look that Kali often reverted to and, had they not grown out she would have just kept them as they were. They still looked perfect.

"I am feeling very Autumnal, Carly! Give me something seasonal, please!" Kali enthusiastically asked.

"I have just the thing for you, it just came in this week and I only just unboxed it today. Hang on…" Carly returned with a little bottle and shaking it towards her friend said "Pumpkin Spice. This one has your name all over it!"

She opened the bottle and showed Kali the colour.

"Oh my, that is dreamy. Yes please!"

Carly started filing her nails and removing the old manicure before starting the new one. Before long

Carly was on seamless autopilot as the manicure was taking place, the girls chatting away as they always did.

"Speaking of Pumpkin Spice, have you been to that new place in town" Kali asked Carly as she switched filing to another finger. "I went in the other day and it was DELICIOUS!"

"Oh, I know, ever since you posted about it, I have gone in every day before work!" as she picked up her empty "I Like You a Latte" cup and shook it towards Kali. "I didn't even know it existed until I seen your post and now it's like, my new addiction!"

"Aw I should have brought you another one down today, I was just so busy this morning I never had the chance to pop down first" admitted Kali. "Are you free sometime this week and we can maybe go get one together?"

Kali left her nail appointment with stunning new Pumpkin Spice nails, and the promise of a mate-date on Tuesday with one of her closest friends. She had a little spring in her step as she walked back towards the car, admiring the nude-orangey-brown polish that glossed her nails. The perfect colour to match her favourite season!

Kali parked her sleek-black Range Rover in her spot on her double drive-way and carefully shut her door, taking care not to damage her nails and headed to her front door as the car automatically locked. She held her fob to her front door to unlock it and before she even stepped a foot inside the vestibule, Hugo was twirling and dancing to see her. She scooped him up and through the side of her eye she noticed a "we tried to deliver your parcel" note from the delivery driver.

Due to the number of packages that she receives daily, she had invested in a parcel drop box which had been a God-send. In the two months that she had it she had never had to collect a parcel so she was a little annoyed that she had to go to the neighbour's house to pick one up.

She placed her keys down on the sideboard, catching a whiff of her Jo Malone diffuser and a sight of herself in her grand round mirror. She loved wearing beiges, browns and creams as it complimented her tan. She kept it up all year round with a continuous regime of exfoliation, application and removal. She revelled in this part of her self-care routine. Back when she was a teenager, she used to use the cheapest tans available, always opting for the darkest option to look better and last longer. Or so she thought! It used to stain her clothes and bedding and it always smelled like some kind of strange stale biscuits. As the tan wore off, it would leave gravelly patches on her skin and would take forever to fully remove. Being a typical teenager, she wouldn't wait or scrub it off, but instead just re-apply more on top. It would make her a range of patchy colours, light, dark, and even orange in a few places.

Now she was much more skilled in the art of fake tanning. She took the time, and the process was much more enjoyable now that she was using high-end brands that smelled of luxury. She'd play her favourite music, light a candle and take time to apply the lotions and creams, paying particular attention to her elbows, knees, hands and feet. Through experience, and a multitude of online tutorials she learned that this was the key to it looking like a real sun tan. And it wasn't the darkest of darks that she used now it was soft, subtle golden glow. Just enough for her onlookers to wonder where she'd been to top up her tan.

She put on Hugo's checked harness and lead for a wander round the block, with the delivery note in her pocket to collect the parcel on the way back. As beautiful as the neighbourhood was, due to the size and grandeur of the houses most of their owners were successful and out at work a lot of the time. There was no typical neighbourhood feeling to the place. The houses were lit up with show-off lights and the drives were decorated with fancy cars. But no children played on the streets. There was no one playing Kerby like they used to back in the day, bouncing the ball off the curbs. There was no ice cream vans and children scrambling home for money before they missed it. There were no games of hide and seek and kids shouting "games-up-the-poley." All of the things she remembered from her childhood neighbourhood were simply not there. There was no atmosphere to the most sought-after area in town and Kali had never noticed it before, but now she did it felt strangely quiet.

She took a deep breath as she embraced herself, ready to walk up the professionally landscaped front garden of her neighbour. Although they had lived in the house for a few years, she realised that she did not know who even lived in the house only two doors down from her own. She stepped on each white rectangular paving stone like the stepping stones they were somewhat loosely based on and approached the front door. It was identical to every other door on the street. It was anthracite grey with a silver minimal, yet statement, door handle. The only difference being the writing on the name plaque: Smythe.

Chapter 10

Emma

Emma sensed that the atmosphere in her work place was getting worse. Everyone was scared to step a foot out of line for fear of getting in trouble. The radio was no longer on as the food was prepared, the chatter and giggle between the girls no longer happened during clean up. Everyone just came in, done their job and then went back home. It had been like that since the start of the term.

Then, one day, as she plated up a little boy in Primary 4's food with a smile as always, he turned around and walked to his table. But as he did, the plate slipped from his hands and smashed onto the floor. The plate shattered and the chicken and gravy went everywhere. In that very second, she started to plate up the food to replace it for him but she stopped in her tracks as the usually calm head teacher turned round and scolded him in front of everyone. The blood raged in her face as she scowled at the poor little boy, and then as quick as it happened, she left the dinner hall. He was in shock: yes, he'd been shouted at before but never like that, and not in front of everyone. Every other child in the school was staring at him in disbelief. He was so shocked and embarrassed that he ran to the toilets and locked himself in a cubicle. It took one of the support staff 10 minutes to convince him to come out and eat his lunch.

When he finally returned to the dinner hall, his friends put their supportive arms around his shoulders as he walked back to the table. Emma gave him another plate of hot food and the mess had long been cleaned up. A few minutes later and it was like it never even happened.

Emma continued on in silence as she washed the dishes and put away everything ready for another day tomorrow. Even Julie, who was always known to be a bit of a chatterbox and up for a laugh worked the rest of the day in almost complete silence. At the end of her shift, Emma picked up her personal belongings and said good-bye to the girls. Instead of heading straight home to prepare the tea as she usually would, she went to the bakery and picked up something to eat for a very rare treat. After the little incident today, she wanted her children to know that no matter when bad things happen, good things are always around the corner. They just had to keep going.

Their little faces lit up as they seen the little white and blue paper bags. It wasn't often they were able to get such treats on a random weeknight. The warm sausage rolls filled their bellies and the custard that oozed from the donuts caused absolute sheer delight! Because of the extra time they had due to the early tea, she called Dan and told him to meet them at the park. The kids were playing on the playground as their father arrived, and he enjoyed his now lukewarm tea as much as he would have if it was still piping hot. After a quick chase around the park, Emma pulled out the frisbee from her bag. The girls loved to cheat by passing it between themselves, acting as though they were one player split in two. It was hard to guess what they were going to do next. Then, just as she was sure they were about to pass it to Dan, they threw it to her so intentionally poorly that she'd never have a chance of catching it. Jasper was wise to their ways and went between them to catch the frisbee and pass it on safely to his mum and dad. The laughter that erupted from each of the Millars was infectious, they couldn't help but laugh at the fun they were making.

When the game finished, they all strolled home together. Dan squeezed Emma's hand in appreciation for the little random night of family fun. Fern placed her tiny hand in hers as she glanced down, she saw Luna grab Fern's other hand. She smiled down at them as a tear welled in her eye. As different as they were with blonde straight hair and blue eyes, and red curly hair and green eyes, they complimented each other like Yin and Yang. She looked over to Dan and he had his arm round Jasper's shoulders and in that moment everything was perfect. The Millars walked through the park all together in a line spanning the width of the path. She had so much fun with her little family that she even forgot to take a picture of it.

Emma loved photographs, and although she rarely printed or posted them, she had tens of thousands of them on her phone. Later, it disappointed her a little that she wouldn't have evidence of the memory to look back on. But that night in bed she kept playing the image over and over in her head so that she'd never forget it. Emma went to sleep that night, for the first time in a long time, feeling content.

At work the next day, the air had shifted. She couldn't quite decide if it was better or worse at first. Rumour had it that the head teacher hadn't returned after the dinner hall shouting incident and would be off for at least 2 more weeks. Emma decided that if the main negative force of the school was gone, then things could only get better. Surely it was the Head Teachers fault that she felt intimidated and inferior every time she seen her.

She was wrong. Things got progressively worse over the following week or so. Not only had any fun atmosphere all but evaporated, the structure and routine began to fall around the school like bricks from a derelict house on a rural hill. People would turn up for meetings that no one was aware of. Classes would turn up for assemblies that hadn't been planned. And slowly, but surely, she noticed a change in the behaviour of the children. The pleases and thank you's started to go a-miss. More children were sent to SLT office for fighting in the playground or being rude to a staff member. In such a short space of time, the school was almost unrecognisable.

Rumour had it that the teaching and support staff's Wednesday night meeting wasn't just any old regular meeting, but a crisis meeting. Mrs Smythe was to be off for another month until the end of term, and SLT raised concerns that things could not continue the way they were. Brainstorming ideas began to take place, and teachers volunteered to take on leadership responsibilities to help. They also took the time to share the practices that could make the workload more manageable. The teachers aired their feelings about how work was just now, and that they also needed to see improvements in how the school was run. The minutes were drawn up and circulated to all staff, detailing the actions required and whose responsibility they were.

The reason Emma received a copy, was because there were some actions that were the responsibility of all staff. The main ones being:

To be consistent with greetings - maintain a positive attitude which will show the children what is expected of them.

To ensure that good manners are used at all times. If they are forgotten, remind the children of what should be said.

To help and support your colleagues whenever possible.

At first, she scoffed at the minutes. Why was it her responsibility to do any of this? She wasn't even invited to the meeting in the first place. Her job was to follow the recipes and produce healthy meals for the children of the school. But the more she thought about it, the more she realised that they were right. If she didn't uphold the standards expected of the school, then why would the children? She vowed to herself then and there that she would put the radio on as she prepared the meals, and giggle with her friends at work again, just as she used to. She wanted to try hard to be the person she wanted to be for the children, and for her own children. If the positive atmosphere was no longer in the school, then she was going to create it. At least, in her own little way in the dinner hall.

Chapter 11

Nicola

The doorbell went at 4.30pm, and unusually Nicola was at home at this time on Monday afternoon. The boys were at afterschool club until 6pm but she just could not last another minute at work so she came home for some much needed space and time alone. However, the universe had other ideas. The doorbell had gone twice in the space of half an hour. For the Smythe's, that was unheard of. No one ever came to the door unless it was a Sunday and it was their turn to host the family get together.

She had been sitting on the armchair in silence with a cup of coffee and was annoyed that she had to get up. Again. She stomped to the door and answered to a young woman standing there, full of make-up and a little dog.

"Yes?" she asked rudely as she glared up and down at the girl, thinking she was here to sell something.

"Sorry to bother you" the girl replied, holding up a delivery note. "I think my parcel was delivered here?"

She was so caught up in her own thoughts that it took her a second or two to click that the parcel delivered just 30 minutes before belonged to this woman, who must have been her neighbour. She glanced her up and down again, wondering how someone so young could possibly afford a house up here. Then she realised that she must still live with her mother. With that thought, she humphed as she picked up the parcel "Oh, here" and thrust it into the girl's arms before shutting the door in her face.

Nicola could hardly contain her tears. She sat back down in the chair and cried big, fat sobs as tears ran down her face. At lunchtime she was called in to a meeting with Jamie's school to discuss what was going on and any support they could offer. She was absolutely mortified. A head teachers' son in trouble at school for being disrespectful and being offered support! How could this happen to her? She manages home and school efficiently. She has always been respected for it. Her reputation precedes her wherever she goes in her local education circle. *How humiliating,* she sobbed. She did not want to show her face in work again.

The tears streamed down her face as she wept for the difficulty of life; how work was chaotic and no one was doing anything right. She cried for her home life; how her children seemed to hate her; how no one done anything and everything was left to her; she cried for her husband who was always away and left her to deal with it all.

It's not that James didn't care. He was very supportive and offered a listening ear whenever she needed it and provided advice as soon as she asked for it. It's just that he was too far away to do anything to physically help. He spoke to his sons on the phone and told them that it wasn't fair what they were doing to their mum. He tried his best to give her side of the story and make them realise the impact of their actions. But they just did not listen. Or at least, if they did, they took no action and nothing changed.

The stress on her started to penetrate through over-whelmed and over-exhausted, she found it difficult to fall asleep. And, when she eventually did, she would toss and turn all night and had all sorts of awful dreams. Most days, she woke up more tired than she was when she went to bed.

After almost two weeks of not sleeping, falling out with her children, a messy house, and a difficult time at school, it all came to a head with an incident in the dinner hall. A child dropped his plate and it smashed on the floor. She lost her temper and raised her voice at him for being so careless whilst the whole school stared at her in stunned silence. This was not the Mrs Smythe that they knew. That moment, Nicola knew she'd had enough and could no longer cope with the pressures. She picked up her personal belongings and headed straight to her car. On her way home she bit the bullet and made a doctor appointment for the following morning. Something she knew was coming but had been covering it up with an Elastoplast and kept putting it off.

The next day, for the first time in her life, Nicola called in sick to work. She had an appointment at 10.30am, and after dropping the kids off at breakfast club, she headed home and poured herself a strong coffee to keep her awake. The tears yet again were welling up in her eyes, and as she blinked, they cascaded down her cheeks like a steady waterfall. She thought of what she was going to say to her GP. She tried to think of all of the different ways she had been dealing with her situation. So far, she had tried the reasoning route. That did not work. The boys just couldn't see her point of view and only retorted with their own. Then she tried the shouting, disciplinarian route. That didn't work either. All that happened was the boys put their walls up and it seemed to only make matters worse. She tried to ignore the situation, but the mess just piled up and it made it impossible to be anywhere on time or have anything done. She struggled to think what else she could do to make the situation any better. With that thought, she took a gulp of her coffee and dosed off in the arm chair until her reminder woke her up.

She poured another coffee into her travel mug and headed off to the doctor's surgery.

"Hello Mrs Smythe, long time, no see! What can I do you for?" said Dr Rasheed very efficiently, as she scoured her previous history on the computer.

"It is very embarrassing, and I don't know where to start..." she stared down at the tissue she was fumbling with and used it to catch a tear as it fell off of her cheek. "But everything just seems to be going wrong. I feel completely out of control."

"Ok" nodded Dr Rasheed as she prompted further explanation.

"My kids have changed completely almost overnight. I can no longer cope with the housework – my house is constantly messy. And work, that used to be my absolute passion but now I cannot bear to be in the place anymore." By now the tears were streaming down her face. "And I am just. So. Tired. But for the life of me I cannot sleep."

After a lengthy discussion, well, as lengthy as you can have in a 10 minute appointment, she was signed off work for 2 weeks and prescribed some medication to take. She was hesitant to take it, believing that people like her did not get depressed or have mental health issues. But the Doctor explained that sometimes a little help is needed to help us cope with the pressures of life and help balance our mental health. She explained that people from all walks of life take anti-depressants and she wasn't the first, and certainly won't be the last professional person to ever be prescribed antidepressants.

Before she could change her mind, she headed straight to the pharmacy and handed in her prescription. She was so anxious she couldn't just sit and wait the 20 minutes she was told it would take to prepare, so she jumped into her car and headed to the local coffee shop drive through. She ordered the largest, strongest coffee they had, and by the time she got back to the pharmacy her prescription was ready.

The drive home was a blur. She was in autopilot as she navigated the roads in a daze. She placed her keys on the kitchen table, noting the dent that happened when everything first went wrong. She pulled out a chair and sat down, staring at the box of medicine deciding what to do with it. She opened the box and took out the blister pack of green and yellow capsules. Normally, she would read the information leaflet front to back before taking any medicine. But everything that she done normally was no longer working for her.

So without any other consideration she popped the pill from its pack and swallowed it with a swig of her coffee.

The relief of taking a positive step in the right direction washed over her as she lay on the sofa with a blanket. She closed her eyes and slept for 5 hours straight. The most she had slept in ages. Even after three strong coffees and an anti-depressant.

Chapter 12

Ten days had passed since Nicola had her breakdown. Ten days of anti-depressants. Ten days of the jitters and nausea whilst her body began to settle into the new drug that was supposed to help her. But so far, things felt much worse. It's like all of the stresses she had been juggling for so long just dropped to the ground with a thud, and with it came an inability to function. Days turned to night, and nights turned to day. She spent most of the time in bed either comatose or with tears streaming down her face. Her body simply did not have the energy for the sobbing that she had recently come accustomed to.

With their mother shut in her bedroom 24/7, and their father at work down south, Jamie and Nicholas were forced to do everything and keep the house running. It's not that they didn't try to rouse their mother, they tried multiple times. But she was either sleeping, incoherent in her speech, or just blanked them like they weren't even there. No longer did they have someone reminding them of all the things they had to do. No one to do their washing or make them meals. No one to drop them off and pick them up. No one to run around after them to make sure all of their needs were met. They had no choice but to look after themselves. At 12 and 13 years old, they were more than capable of walking the 20 minutes to school. They could butter their own bread and make their own packed lunches. They could stick a pizza or chicken nuggets in the oven. And although they didn't want to do any of it, they had no choice. If they didn't cook – they wouldn't eat. If they didn't walk to school, they wouldn't go. And if they didn't do their own washing, then they would have nothing to wear. There was only a couple of times Jamie could pick up his clothes off of the floor and re-wear them before they started to smell. And he did not like that one bit.

As two weeks had passed since she started her medicine and got her sick line from the doctor, it dawned on her that she was not ready to return to work. She picked up her phone for the first time in a long time and popped it on charge, and when it had enough battery, she called the doctor's surgery and made a telephone appointment made for that very afternoon. Her legs alone didn't have enough strength to stand up and get out of bed so she steadied herself with one hand on her bedside table and the other on the bed post. She edged one foot into her slipper, the familiar warm fluffy cavern which usually made her feel comfort felt cold and foreign. It was strange having something on her feet other than the sheets of her duvet. Still holding onto her bed post, she slid in her other foot and scuttled towards her bedroom door. As it opened, the light streamed in and she had to shield her eyes as they adjusted. Spending over a week in a darkened room with the curtains drawn made this sudden step into day light almost blinding. She grasped the hand rail and felt its smoothness as she ran her hands over it as her feet slowly, shakily, reached for each step.

The kitchen wasn't how it was usually left. There was clutter on the surfaces, the kettle had been pulled out and there was toast crumbs all around the toaster. It was all a bit over-whelming as she tried to piece together what had happened to her immaculate kitchen. She filled the kettle, went to her fridge for the milk. As she opened the door, her tummy started to grumble and she searched for something to eat. There wasn't much, but now she seen them, eggs were exactly what she fancied. She placed two in a pot, filled it with water and heated them up to a boil. She opened her pantry cupboard and reached in for the bread but she couldn't feel it. She drew open the cupboard a little farther and peered inside. There was none. The cupboard was almost bare. She looked through the rest of the cupboards and seen that all the tins had been used up. The freezer which was normally jam packed with home-made batch cooked meals healthy and a mix of healthy convenience foods had more ice in it than food. She hadn't realised she'd let things go this much.

When her coffee was ready, she sat down at the table and pulled out her phone from the pocket of her dressing gown. *If I can't go shopping, then we will need to get the shopping brought to us,* she thought in a moment of clarity. She went onto her favourite supermarket and set up her first ever online shop. The first available slot was in two days-time and she set it up so that the same order would come every week thereafter. *That should do me, until I start to feel better,* she thought. Normally, she would never do an online shop. She worried that the staff wouldn't take the care she did when choosing the best quality ingredients for her meals. *It would only be for a couple of weeks* she thought, and with that, the order was placed.

She served up her eggs with a little salt, and nothing else since there wasn't much anyway. Just as well, as the two eggs were more than enough for her. It was the first substantial thing she had to eat since the day of the incident at school. As she tried to push the memory away from her mind, she felt an overwhelming wave of tiredness wash over her. She got to her feet and set her alarm 10 minutes before her telephone appointment, and just about made it to the sofa before she passed out.

The alarm startled her as it rang louder and louder. She couldn't figure out what the noise was or where it came from at first. She finally located her phone back on the dining room table and managed to turn it off. She made her way to the sink and ran the water with her fingers under it and the jitters were as bad as they had ever been. She filled a glass and brought it straight to her mouth. As she gulped down the water, she felt the coldness radiate from the centre of her throat outwards. It almost took her breath away.

Suddenly, she had the desire to be outside in the fresh air. She opened her bi-fold doors that led from the kitchen and stepped out onto the patio, tilting her head towards the sky. The rain lightly fell gently on her face, down her neck and ran down onto her chest. Usually, she would run from the rain, but now, in this moment, she embraced it. She felt every rain drop as it lightly landed on her skin, every droplet that raced down her skin. And within minutes she was drenched. Almost forgetting the time, she stepped inside and grabbed a tea towel. She wiped her face and neck and scrunched her hair with it in an attempt to squeeze out most of the rainwater. As she did, her phone rang and with a deep breath, she sat down at the table and spoke to her doctor.

After explaining how she was getting on, or more to the point, how she wasn't; with countless days in bed, the nausea and shakes, and zero appetite, Dr Rasheed decided that a 4 week line should be enough time for the medicine to be fully working. Knowing that she had more time to recover and that she might be able to start to pull herself together, she hung up the phone as the relief washed over her. She smiled for the first time in a long time.

Whilst she was on a roll, she went upstairs and took a long, hot shower. It was a stark contrast to the shower she'd had in the garden only a few minutes before. But the water felt so good as it lightly stung her arms and chest. She faced the water flow and let it bounce off her face, leaving her gasping for air whenever she could. She washed her hair, massaging her scalp with her finger tips as the smell of lavender and orange filled her senses and the shower cubicle. As she combed through her conditioner with her fingers, her hair had never felt smoother. Its slick, glossy strands weaving through her fingers from root to tip. After lathering up her whole body and rinsing it off, she stood as the water battered the top of her back and it almost felt like a massage. She had no idea how long she'd been in the shower, but the water started to cool and she noticed her fingertips had wrinkled. She turned the shower off and stepped out of the cubicle suddenly feeling dizzy. She sat on the toilet seat with her towel draped around her and fumbled to dry herself a bit. Exhausted from the events of the day, she stumbled straight back into bed.

As the days went on, she found that she was more awake during the day. Things seemed to take a flip turn when she went to bed, she found that she now had difficulty falling asleep. Just as well James wasn't there often, as he probably wouldn't sleep very much either. This was something that she was not used to. Her busy life-style and always being on the go meant that when she finally stopped, sleep would snatch her from reality so quickly that she never even noticed that she was falling asleep until her alarm went off in the morning, ready to do it all over again.

She became a shell of the woman she once was - too tired during the day to do anything remotely productive, and too consumed by her thoughts at night to sleep. It was a vicious cycle and not one she knew how to even begin to break. She'd tried to drink coffee during the day to make her more alert. She'd tried drinking camomile tea at bedtime to help relax her but the only impact they seemed to make was on her toilet visiting frequencies through both day and night. She felt embarrassed with herself that she got herself into this mess. Only a matter of weeks ago she was running a whole school, hundreds of pupils and staff relied on her. Her own family relied on her. And here she was, an absolute mess who couldn't distinguish day from night. Who had zero levels of energy and productivity. Who barely felt human at all.

The next day was another bad day. She felt so bad about how her life had deteriorated so quickly that the dark, cold depression engulfed her. She had no desire or motivation to even attempt to get out of bed at all. She hadn't been to the toilet. She hadn't eaten or drank anything. She could barely open her eyes. She did not know what day it was, never mind if it was day or night time. As she struggled to lift her heavy eye lids, she reached for her bedside glass of water and drew it to her lips, only to discover that it was bone dry. As she opened her mouth an awful stale stench of a couple of days-worth of morning breath accumulated, and she started to dry wretch. Instead of getting herself a glass of water from the ensuite literally less than 10 steps from her bed. She just rolled over and cried until she fell asleep in her own stench as a puddle of grief made a halo on her pillow.

James returned home from work early and as he caught sight of his wife, he threw his hands up to his mouth in an attempt to stop the uncontrollable sobs. He knew things were bad, but he did not realise just how ill his wife was. Nicola was naturally a slender person. She didn't have to work hard on her figure like lots of other people did. She ate generally well and enjoyed light exercise at her gym on a Saturday. That was it, but it was enough to keep her in shape. Her figure had barely altered in the 20 years that they had been together, despite everything they had been through – growing and birthing two children, promotions in both of their careers, and multiple long stints flying the parenting plane solo as her husband was on detachment for months at a time. Nicola was a strong person with a personality to match. But as James stared at his wife, she looked weak and frail and had aged years in a matter of weeks. She lay in bed like a bag of bones. Her skin looked saggy and dull with dehydration and her unbrushed hair resembled a bird's nest. He was shocked to see his ever-immaculate wife in such a bad way.

The next morning, instead of cutting the grass, polishing his car and a round of golf with his friends as was his normal Saturday routine, James called round multiple agencies and found ads to search for something to help at home. James knew that Nicola prided herself on a clean, well-run home and thought that relieving the pressure for her would no doubt help. After around an hour of searching and numerous phone calls, he found a suitable cleaner who could fit the Smythe's in with hours that would suit. Her reviews were impeccable, lots of praise and regular clients. Not wanting to humiliate his wife in any way, he explained that she is a very house-proud person, but is ill just now and asked her not to disturb her. Safe in the trust that she was kind and helpful, James set up a weekly direct-debit and arranged for her to come every Monday. He knew that by taking this pressure of his wife, it would make things a little better. He knew that hiring a cleaner might only be the very tip of the ice-berg of what else needed to be done to help.

That night James took the boys to the local driving range. Not because he missed his golf that day, but because he knew with him being away the boys must have had a tough time of it lately. As much as Nicola liked to delegate, she was not one to ask for help, ever, and the state she was in right now, he knew she wouldn't have been capable of doing so even if she wanted to. The boys had said to their father that mum wasn't well, but they didn't say how bad things actually were. He knew that they had been playing up for their mum and that it had upset her, but to actually see that the boys had been caring for themselves, he felt sorry for them. He also felt proud of how they had stepped up to the plate and how they had managed without the support of their parents. He was determined now, more than ever, that a night out of the house having fun would do them all a world of good.

The drive to the range was silent. James tried to lighten the mood by telling them stories of his week at work and even tried to pull some dad jokes. But Jamie and Nicholas just hung their heads down. Suspicion ran through them as to why dad would be treating them to something so good when they had behaved so poorly and caused all of this to happen. The boys went through the motions; they hit the ball when it was their turn, and cheered and clapped whenever someone done well, or boo-ed when they didn't. All the while, they were waiting on their father to scold them as the guilt seeped from their pores. But he never did. The hurt that they had caused their mother was too great for them to enjoy themselves and the three of them returned home in the silence in which they arrived.

James' boys' night did not have the effect that he was sure it would. He couldn't understand it. The boys had been through so much, that they couldn't even enjoy themselves on a treat night with their own father. And then the thought hit him like lightning strikes the tallest tree in the field – with a sudden catastrophe. Perhaps they were angry at him for abandoning them all their lives. He had never, ever once felt like that. Because of the job that James had, he was able to provide his family with things that he knew they wouldn't have otherwise. They had one of the biggest, best houses in the whole city. They went to a private school to get the best education possible so that they could achieve their full potential in life. They went to every club and social event possible, creating a width and breadth of experiences that many are not fortunate enough to get.

For the first time as an adult, James felt as though he had failed his family. He could see through his suddenly darkened rose-tinted glasses that perhaps things weren't as advantageous as he once thought they were. His children did not have the father they needed or deserved. He was hardly ever there. And now, their mother was slipping through their fingers too. The guilt consumed him and once again, James found himself with tears rolling down his cheeks. He couldn't ever remember a time he cried as an adult and in the space of one day, he found himself inconsolable for the second time.

Chapter 13

Kali

Usually on Sundays Kali and Michael would spend the day together. She made sure that all of her work for the week was tied up on a Saturday so that she and Michael could spend a whole day of quality time together. But this weekend, and for the second weekend in a row, Michael had to work, He was becoming more and more successful in his role that his workload increased so much and he struggled to fit the job into his contracted hours. He had reports to complete and videos to record and edit to upload to his works social media before Monday morning meaning that Sunday was the only chance he had to do so.

As much as she supported Michael's career, she didn't care too much for the fact that she had to spend another Sunday lonely. It's not that she was alone, as such, she had her family and friends and literally thousands of followers to spend her time on, but not having Michael with her just made her feel a little bit empty.

Despite their busy lives, Sundays was always "their" day. They caught up with family for breakfast, or went on long walks, or went shopping or went out for dinner. Sometimes they didn't get dressed at all and brought the duvet down to the sofa and snuggled up binge-watching series on Netflix. It didn't matter to her what they done, as long as it was spent together but today, it was just Kali and Hugo. She followed her usual morning routine of vitamins, yoga, smoothie and a book. After all that was done, she found herself at a loose end and called her mum for a chat and they arranged to have lunch together later.

After a walk around the park with Hugo, she jumped in the shower and decided to dress up a little bit for their wee day out. Thirty minutes in the dressing room later, she emerged looking effortlessly cool in her black leather-look leggings, over-sized beige knitted cashmere sweater, and her chunky matt Doc Marten boots. She wore a #gifted Katie Loxton snap-shot style cross-body bag with a leopard print strap. It was the most patterned, colourful thing she would ever wear but it complemented her neutral vibes with a pop of fun which is exactly the type of day she planned: effortlessly cool and calm with a hint of excitement.

Kali loved spending time with her mum. She had always been so kind and supportive in whatever she wanted to do; she was her biggest cheerleader. Perhaps this is why she never gave up on anything, she knew that she would be supported no matter what. If something ever went wrong, her mum advocated saying that it wasn't failure, just a bump in the road, and she loved her for it. She would treat her mum whenever she could, and today was the perfect opportunity.

She walked the 30 minutes to her parents' house. She knew that she would more than likely have a few cocktails today, so wanted to get in as many steps as possible before then. As she cut through the park, she noticed a familiar face walking towards her, but couldn't work out who it was. She assumed it must have been one of her online followers, so as she got close to her, she smiled. But the woman's eyes grew and darted around in a panic looking left to right, before she lowered her head and continued walking as they passed each other. *Strange* thought Kali, as she scrambled her brain trying to figure out what all that was about. A lightbulb went on in her head and she realised that it was that horrible neighbour, Mrs Smythe.

Why she was so rude and flustered, she had no idea, but Kali knew that that was only her second ever encounter with her and she had done nothing but collect a parcel and smile at her. Rather than worry about it, it just wasn't in her nature, she knew she had done nothing wrong to her and that it must be her problem, so she continued her walk to her mothers with a spring in her step.

Sharon opened the door with a kiss and a hug and was, as always. happy to see her daughter. She thought of how hard Kali had worked to get where she was and beamed with pride at the woman she had become.

"Go and put on some lippy, Mum. I am taking you somewhere nice!" Sharon giggled as she knew only too-well that meant that some alcohol was going to be consumed this afternoon.

As Sharon came downstairs with a sweep of lipstick, a spritz of perfume and a change of earrings later, Kali handed her a glass of prosecco.

"Let's start this day as we mean to go on! You look beautiful, mum."

"Och you" Sharon playfully hit her daughter's arm and took a swig of the cold fizz. "Your dad is busy in the garden anyway. I am sure he won't miss me too much!"

After the bottle of prosecco, her dad dropped them both off in the city centre. "Don't have too much fun, you two," he called after them as they linked arm and arm and crossed the street.

After a few hours shopping, both women had a few carrier bags each filled with new clothes and accessories to add to their ever-growing collections.

"Kali, I am getting a little bit thirsty!" giggled Sharon to her daughter. The pair of them looked at each other, linked arms again and headed along to Miller & Carters. Luckily, they managed to get a table without a reservation. They ordered a cocktail each, and as it arrived Kali took a video of their cheers, tagging the restaurant in it.

If you weren't part of the pair, it would have been hard to keep up with the conversation. If her dad were here, he would have bowed out long-before as the topics whizzed from shopping to nosey neighbours to catching up with friends to family ups and downs and everything else in between. They started to talk about all the funny things she done as a child, and how everyone always commented that she was the cutest little baby. She would often strip and put on the weirdest combination of clothes, stripey tights, spotty tops and tartan cardigans, finished off with a pair of wellies and ear muffs.

"Oh darling, you have lit up every room you've been in since the day you were born!" her mum gushed. "Have you and Michael thought about having any children yet?"

It was a question she knew she probably shouldn't ask but she never really mentioned the idea before and she just wanted to know if being a grandmother was likely to be in her future at all.

"You know mum, it's not something that's a priority right now. We are still so young, and we are committed on focusing on our careers right now."

Kali noticed that her mum looked a little disappointed.

"Maybe, one day, there would be the pitter patter of tiny baby feet in the house, but just not right now."

"I would love nothing more than to be a granny" said Sharon bashfully.

"I know mum, and you would be the best! But it's just not something that's in our plans right now."

A short silence fell over the pair but the thoughtful stillness was interrupted with another round of cocktails being delivered by the waiter.

"Drinks, from the boss, on the house" he smiled as he placed the drinks down.

"Oh, thank you so much! Why?!" questioned Sharon to the waiter.

He just gave a little wink towards the pair and turned on his heel to serve the next table. Sharon turned to Kali with her jaw dropped in question. She picked up her phone and waved it toward her mum, showing her the post that she uploaded only 20 minutes before.

"Three thousand likes on our post, Mum!"

"Oh my gosh! Already?!" Sharon was shocked that that many people cared what she and her daughter were up to.

She explained to her mum, again, that by sharing businesses on her platform, it benefits them, as well as her. She told her mum how she had got her new bag sent to her in the post free of charge the other week, and today was her first day wearing it. She said she would also share a picture of her outfit later and tag the business as a thank you for sending her the gift. She didn't always do that, though. She was sent so many free items, and she just did not have the time. Even if she did, she only shared businesses she truly liked. She prided herself on it. Lots of people in her field take on any job for the money, but that just wasn't her thing.

"I love your new bag, Kali. It's so nice. I can't believe you got that for free!"

She looked down at the leopard print strap. "It is lovely, Mum. You can just have it!"

"Do not be daft" Sharon exclaimed!

"Mum, its brand new, and I have hundreds of bags!" Kali thought about how she was going to take it off after their day out and give her it right then and there.

"I was meaning you could get me a similar one for my birthday, it is only next month" she smirked as a reminder.

And with that, she had an idea. Just like her daughter, Sharon also had a thing for bags. The ultimate luxury in handbags was her LV Neverfull. It was one of the first luxury items she saved up and put money aside for off of her influencer income. She worked so hard for it but she knew that her mother more than deserved one. With a smirk, she made a mental note to pick one out in the morning for her mother's birthday.

After an afternoon of cocktails, shopping and giggles, her dad came to collect them. He was playing the same songs he always did, and she smiled to herself as she thought of all of the memories these songs brought with them and caught his eye in the mirror. He winked a friendly, loving wink towards his daughter.

"Thank you so much for today, sweetheart. Though you really didn't need to pay for all that. I am more than happy to just spend some nice time with you." Sharon took Kali's hand in hers.

And with that, Kali emptied her purse, phone, lip gloss and comb out of her bag and handed it to her mum. "Here you go, mum."

"Kali! My birthday isn't for another month yet" as she pushed it back towards her daughter.

"No way, mum! It was free. You're not getting that for your birthday. I just want you to have it." and with a smile, she handed it to her mum.

"You're some girl, Kali Munro!"

Kali smiled back. "Do you want to pop in for a wee cup of tea?"

Her parents sat on the sofa and had a cuddle with Hugo. Michael had not long arrived home after a long day at work, and the 4 of them chatted away while they drank their cups of tea. The timer started to beep for the dinner that Michael had already put on for he and Kali. Sensing their desire to be together, her parents headed off home to enjoy the rest of their Sunday evening and give the two of them some time on their own.

After a brilliant day with her mum, she had achy legs from all the walking and shopping, she was pleased to see that her activity rings for the day were already long closed. Happy-tipsy with the cocktails, she and Michael cuddled in on the sofa for the rest of the night and watched two films back to back. One action, then one rom com. Just as they always liked to do.

It was the perfect wee day and Kali was feeling so blissfully content, that she just closed her eyes and fell asleep in her perfect wee bubble.

Chapter 14

Nicola

Nicola did not even hear that someone was in her house, nor did she hear them pottering about, lifting things, wiping them down and returning them to their original spot. She did not hear the hoover as it glided across the carpets. She did not hear the scrubbing of the bath or the showers. Not a thing.

But sometime in the afternoon she awoke and dragged herself down the stairs. An unfamiliar smell tickled her nostrils as she tried to figure out what it was. Then she realised that her kitchen was clean. Not just regular, Smythe-level clean, but gleaming, actually sparkling. Confused about what was going on, she went through to the living room, and then to the downstairs toilet. Both places were the same - immaculate. A small burst of energy fired up inside her as she scaled the stairs and seen that every room was the same. All of the rooms, except her own. She knew she didn't do it herself. She knew that the boys and James just wouldn't know quite *how* to achieve this level of perfection in the cleaning department. She ran through a variety of emotions. At first, she was happy the house was clean but then she worried about who done it. Was a stranger in her house? How humiliating it would be to have someone come in and clean for her? Was she even safe in her own home anymore? Were the children safe? Did anyone see her? In a state of confusion, she picked up her phone and called James.

After 10 missed calls during his one hour meeting, James finally returned the call to his frantic wife. When he explained that he organised for a weekly clean, the confusion that she felt changed to a rage that fired in her belly and rose to her throat. The words that spat out of her mouth were unrecognisable to James as coming from his wife. She absolutely flipped her lid. She was so flustered and confused and hurt that she could not even explain to James why she was so angry. She just hung up the phone, checked the front and back doors were both locked, and went straight back to bed.

It was after hours of crying and trying to get to sleep that she tried to think of the last time that she felt any happiness that it came to her. She remembered her moments in the garden just a few days earlier as the rain washed over her, and how nice the fresh, cold crisp air felt. She suddenly longed to feel that simple pleasure yet again. She opened her bedroom window as wide as she could and inhaled long, deep breaths as the night air filled her lungs. The silence of the outside world softly lit by streetlights brought her a sense of calm that she had long forgotten. When she finally went to bed, she closed her eyes and drifted off into a peaceful slumber.

That morning she arose and went to the bathroom, washed her face and brushed her teeth. She picked up a set of comfy clothes and put on her trainers with more intention than she'd managed to muster up in the last few weeks. She longed to feel the fresh air inside her lungs again, and soon found herself down at the local park walking through the heavily wooded areas that could be mistaken for a lush forest. With the noise of the wildlife around her and the wind rustling through the trees as the crisp autumnal air began to blow through, she felt her anxiety levels begin to reduce. Pleasant feelings began to rustle up inside her, just as the leaves rustled below her feet.

Soon she found that she could not get enough of her daily walks. Most days she went on multiple, exploring the landscape around her city that she never even knew existed before. Now, it became her lifeline; her reason to get up in the morning. The calmness it made her feel she found she couldn't get anywhere else. The relief as her stress and tensions started to melt away with each step as she strolled through nature. She noticed all the little things around her. Her new pastime brought a new routine into her life. Now she had something to look forward to. The walk burned some energy which meant she was a little hungrier than she had been and with food now in the house with the weekly online shopping delivery, and small appetite starting to build, she was starting to build up her strength. Without realising it she had created herself a little selfcare routine, something she thought she had nailed before but turns out actually nothing she was doing was just for her. She was so busy trying hard to be successful in all areas; trying hard to have the best career, looking good, trying to show that she had the best life with the best house, the best family that she actually forgot about the one person she really needed to please.

Her new day time routine rolled into a night time routine too. Before long she found that she was able to fall asleep much easier at nights. Although she wasn't sleeping the whole way through, she found that her nightmares occurred less and she was getting a little more sleep than she had been before. For the first time in weeks, she felt that she finally might have a little control again over her life.

Chapter 15

Emma

After a few weeks of her vow to improve the atmosphere at work, it really was a case of faking it until you make it for Emma. Things just didn't feel quite right at school. Despite this, she continued to listen to her music and have fun with the children and her colleagues; Julie was always a hoot. Soon the smiles and fun started to return in the kitchens and slowly over time, things started to improve throughout the school; the children's manners were restored, and with them, so were their smiles. A joyful sound of giggles and stories filled the dining hall once again as the children were happier and soon, she found that it was beginning to rub off on her. She and Julie were back to sharing celebrity gossip and stories of their weekends and whatnot. She genuinely didn't know if she was actually still unhappy at work, or if she was happy again. Either way, it was working, and she wanted to keep it that way.

Although the change to a negative workplace didn't actually last for long, only a few weeks, it was enough for her and her colleagues to know that working in an environment like that was not something that could be done long term. Apart from the working hours and the little money she received, there was nothing else keeping her there. She had already considered looking for other jobs and being honest with herself, if there was something else that suited her hours then she would have snapped it up. But now that things started to feel normal again, she was glad of it. The routine and ease of the life she had built for herself was comforting.

At home, now there wasn't the worry of work to contend with, she found herself back into the trap of spending her nights endless doom-scrolling. As a result, dislike for her home became more intense. She spent money she couldn't really afford to on the latest vases and dried flower arrangements, candles and diffusers. She was splurging out on designer wax melts to try and make her home smell amazing, even if it didn't look it. But it still wasn't enough her. She found herself beginning to hate the home that she had so lovingly created with what they could afford. It just wasn't enough for her.

She had always enjoyed her children playing with their toys, knowing that their imaginations were growing as they did. But now, the toys irritated her as they got in the way of her own dreams of the perfect home. She began snapping at the children for making a mess and suddenly they were being told to remove toys that surrounded the edges of the living room.

The kids felt unsettled at their mothers change and they did not see why all of a sudden, their toys were no longer to be left out to be played with later. If they had been aware of what was going on, they would have felt that they didn't belong in their own home, that their existence was bothersome to their own mother. But their ages at 5 and 8 years old meant that they couldn't articulate that or even process it. All they knew was that something was different, and it didn't make them feel good and as a result, they got upset whenever they were asked to do anything. Emma and Dan soon found that they were having to spend more time sorting out issues as their behaviour began to deteriorate.

That day, when she came home from work, she had noticed that Dan had left her some flowers on the sideboard. She went over to them to have a look. *They don't do anything for the room. I wish he'd got some nicer ones;* she thought as she gave them a sniff and left them exactly where she found them. She didn't remove the plastic wrapping and rearrange them as she normally would. They just sat looking sorrily-squint in the vase; unappreciated.

She went through to the kitchen and put on the oven to preheat and went upstairs to put away the dried washing whilst she waited. But all of the washing on the drier was strangely gone. She went through to the kids' bedrooms and the washing on the radiator airers were still there, so she folded it all and went to pop it into the drawers. She sighed frustratedly as she saw that the usually neat clothes organisers had clothes put in each of the compartments all willy-nilly. Emma liked to have the visible part of the clothing facing up and smooth, without a seem or a fold in sight but these clothes they were barely even folded, more just rammed in any way possible. The t-shirts were in the leggings compartment, and vests in the t-shirts and she couldn't help but be annoyed. It just meant she had to pull it all out and start organising it again. Annoyance towards Dan started to bubble away inside her. *Why on Earth would he do this? Just making it bloody harder for me.*

When she finally reorganised the drawers, she put the tea in the oven and set off to collect the kids from school. They were happy to see her and she loved to get their hugs and kisses as they greeted her. As they headed home the kids were starving, asking what was for dinner already. Normally, they would wait until Dan was home before they ate but tonight, she was annoyed at him and didn't particularly want to wait to dine with him. So as soon as tea was ready, she plated it up and she and the kids finished their meal before Dan was even home.

When he came through the front door not much later, she was washing up. She turned to look at him, glared at him and turned back towards the dishes.

"What happened? Did you already eat?" Dan asked as he put his hands on his wife's waist.

She turned and moved away to grab the cloth and started wiping up the worktop. "The kids were hungry."

Dan could sense an annoyed tone so he went to give her a kiss on the cheek to make her feel better. But she was not in the mood; she pulled away and started to dry the dishes.

And with that, Dan went upstairs to take a shower. He wondered if she even noticed the flowers that he bought her. They were still sitting exactly as he'd left them. Surely, if she knew that he'd bought her flowers and helped with the washing she'd be happy?

Dan ate his tea alone for the first time in a long time. Even if she wasn't happy to see him, at least his kids were. He spent his night lying on the floor building Lego with Jasper whilst the girls used the small of his back as a trampoline for their Barbies. When the kids were in bed, she and Dan sat at opposite ends of the sofa. He put on a documentary about cars and Emma spent the night on her phone. Again.

The next day after the kids' swimming lessons, Emma set off with her cleaning bucket filled with all of her cleaning products, cloths and sponges to give the house its big weekly clean. Dan popped his hand into the bucket.

"You'll not be needing this!" he put his hand into the bucket and pulled out the bathroom cleaner. "I cleaned the bathroom for you last night," he smirked.

"You did?" Emma asked. "I noticed that the taps were minging this morning," Emma walked through to the bathroom. "Ewwww and there are hairs all in the corner" her face twisting as she grimaced.

Dan raised his voice at her for probably the first time since they'd known each other "EMMA, ARE YOU KIDDING ME?! IS NOTHING I DO GOOD ENOUGH FOR YOU ANYMORE?!"

She thought about how he could possibly be annoyed at her. It was she who was mad at him! He made the house work harder for her these past couple of days. He bought stupid flowers with money they don't even have, that didn't even go with any of the décor in the house, for God's sake! He wasted her time by putting away all the clothes wrong. He wasted his own time doing half a job cleaning the bathroom so much so that she still had to go behind him and do it all again anyway. And it's not her fault that the kids were hungry and wanted their tea before he was home from work, what did he want her to do?

She stayed downstairs to avoid him, she couldn't be bothered dealing with him today. She poured herself a cup of tea and scrolled her socials for half an hour. Seeing all the perfectly presented corners of the immaculate rooms inspired her to improve her own. So, she spent the night trying to organise and declutter the house and make it look somewhat presentable. Going around the kids tidying up the mess and wiping around them. Whenever another toy was pulled out, her eyes rolled with an over-loud sigh. *Bedtime couldn't come quick enough* she thought.

Strangely, when she was putting the kids to bed. Dan didn't surface to help as he usually did. She done everything by herself, and it only made her more annoyed. *Not only did he make things worse for me, but do I now actually have to do everything myself?* For the very first time, Emma doubted her relationship with Dan, thinking she might be better off without him. She pushed these awful thoughts to the side in her mind. *It's just been a tough couple of days, every marriage goes through times like this. Don't be silly.*

Chapter 16

Kali

Monday morning came round, and Kali's head was fuzzy from all of the cocktails the day before. But that didn't stop her waking up excited. She couldn't stop thinking about treating her mum to a Louis Vuitton. She picked up her phone and within seconds she was scrolling through all of the handbags until she arrived at the classic favourite: The Neverfull.

There were so many options, sizes and colours, but she knew exactly what she was looking for; the large, brown monogrammed one with the beige lining. It was elegant, classy and expensive, exactly what her mother deserved. Just a few clicks, and over one thousand Great British Pounds later, the bag was purchased all before Michael had even finished his shower.

Kali, pleased with herself, but still with a dull head ache, rolled out of bed, put her feet into her slippers and slipped into her dressing gown. She reached for the door, finding her way through barely opened eyes. She slowly walked down the stairs, guiding herself with her hand on the banister. When she got into the kitchen, she reached for a glass and poured some ice cold water from the fridge dispenser. It shocked her throat almost painfully but certainly pleasureful, as she gulped down 2 paracetamol. She put the glass on the side next to the sink and went straight back to bed. A couple more hours won't hurt, she told herself.

By the time Michael was ready to go to work, she was lightly snoring away. He kissed her on the forehead and left for the day.

It was around mid-day that she resurfaced. She glanced at her phone. *12:22?! You've got to be kidding me!* She reached over to feel for Michael, but his side of the bed was long cold. She realised that it was indeed a Monday morning, and Michael would be at work, and silently huffed to herself at the thought of him just sneaking away and not even saying goodbye. Then she got annoyed at herself for missing half of the day already!

She leaned over and opened up her diary to check what was on her to-do list for the day:

Content for Cuisine.
Wash and blow dry.
Content for jewellery brand.

She picked up her trusty Minnie Mouse pen and scored through the content for Cuisine and Jewellery content and moved it over to later in the week. She knew that today was definitely not a day for cooking - this was a day that called for being cooked for. She thought of a takeaway, and with that her tummy started to rumble. As for creating jewellery content, she had an appointment to get her nails done at the end of the week, so it made sense to push that to the side too and wait until her nails were fresh.

That just left her wash and blow dry at Blow and Glow at 2pm. A wave of nausea washed over her. The thought of getting ready for that together with the hunger was almost too much. The only reason she decided to still get her hair done today is because it saved her washing it herself. And she didn't need to create content for this one, it was just one of her monthly upkeep appointments for working with them.

As she sat up, her sore head seemed to return from out of nowhere. Her yoga, smoothie and vitamin breakfast were definitely out of the window today. She pulled on her dressing gown and headed downstairs hoping that there was some thick cut white bread and butter to make herself a plate of toast and a cup of tea to sort her out. But instead, all she could find was a bagel and extra light cream cheese. Still, it was better than nothing. She toasted the bagel and thanked the lord for being lucky enough to have a boiling water tap. She had no desire nor the ability to be able to wait for a kettle to boil. She sipped on a steamy hot mug of sweet tea and washed down another dose of paracetamol as she slathered on the cream cheese. She sat down at the dining room table and took the biggest bite, leaving teeth marks in the cheese. *Mmm,* she thought. In just a few bites, the bagel was gone. And it was not enough. Today was a day for all the carbs.

After a quick shower, and minimal make up, she pulled on a pair of fur-lined leggings and an oversized woollen striped jumper. She pulled up the zip towards her chin and back down again, just enough so that the collar was forced to sit up. She brushed her hair quickly and tied it into a loose pony tail at the nape of her neck.

She slipped her feet into her mini Ugg boots and put on her Gucci sunglasses. She didn't even need to glance in the mirror, she knew everything would look perfect together and bang on trend with this Autumn's fashion.

She checked her watch and realised she had enough time to swing by I Like You a Latte for one of their massive almond and pecan croissants. She'd never had one before, but every time she went in, she eyed them up. Or rather, they eyed her up. They seemed to call out her name on every visit. But today, the calls were louder than before, and she wasn't even anywhere near the shop.

She let Hugo out in the garden for a quick wee before she locked and secured the house and jumped into her Range Rover. Heated seats on, windows open, chill music on. Today was a day for all of the comfort. And carbs, of course.

Luckily, Kali had timed it just right and managed to avoid the lunch time rush. She got a parking space practically right outside the café. She stepped out of the car, walked the few short steps to the café door and the sweet, rich smell of coffee and cake filled her nostrils. She was almost overwhelmed with the sense of pleasure just being there gave her. She ordered 2 of the croissants, and 2 lattes with a shot of sugar free vanilla (trying somewhat to make up for the extra calories she had consumed...and was about to consume).

Just then, she remembered a reel she had seen recently about the impact small acts of kindness can have on people, and so she also asked to pay it forward for someone else to enjoy a coffee on her. Although this was the first time that she done this, every time she ordered from then on, she paid for an extra one. It made her smile knowing that in some way, she could help someone else out. And so, she did. Because she could.

When she got back to the car complete with her tray of steaming hot drinks and goodies, she saw she still had 10 minutes before her appointment. She couldn't wait any longer and opened the brown paper bag to the croissants. She took a big bite, and wrapped it back up, started her engine and made her way to the hairdressers. On the way there, she found that she had taken another bite, and another, and another. Then, all of a sudden, the whole thing had disappeared!

She pulled up outside the hairdressers with a couple of minutes to spare. She decided that she couldn't go in with just one croissant. So, without hesitation, she demolished the second croissant. The whole thing, gone, in record time. She washed it all down with big gulp of the sweet latte and finally felt satisfied. She'd consumed more carbs in less than 2 hours than what she would normally in a whole week.

She looked in the mirror, wiped the sticky, delicious crumbs from her lips with the back of her hand, catching them in the bottom of her jumper like a mini make-shift shopping basket. She carefully stepped down out of the car and shook her jumper releasing the crumbs into the air like a puff of dandelion fairies blown with a wish.

She brushed the remaining evidence from her car seat onto the pavement, and with it, wiped away the guilt she felt for being so greedy. She decided to pretend as though she never bought herself and her hairdresser breakfast at all, as though it never happened.

"Hi Shona, how are you?!" she cuddled her hairdresser and handed her the coffee.

"I can't believe that's been a month already since you were last in!" giggled Shona. "I swear the days are just whizzing by just now!"

"Tell me about it!" she lifted her sunglasses and squinted at the bright lights "Oh" and put them back down.

"Are you ok, Kali?!"

"Shona, don't…haha!" She laughed as she tried to explain herself. "I took my mum out yesterday and had a bit too much fun. I am feeling a tad delicate today!"

"Well just you relax, close your eyes and we can have a wee silent appointment today if you want?" Shona offered.

"Oh really, is that a thing?" Kali was amazed.

"Yes, not that anyone has ever wanted one before! But I'd love to try it. I've heard nothing but good things!"

"That would be lovely, actually. Are you sure you wouldn't mind?"

"Not at all! We can catch up another time. Let's give it a go!

She finally removed her sunglasses and closed her eyes as she felt Shona work her magic. With every stroke of the brush, she started to feel a little bit better.

"Ok, I'll just take you over to the sinks now" spoke Shona in barely more than a whisper.

The feeling of the almost too hot water as it ran over her scalp made her feel as though she was in heaven. The savoured sensation of Shona's finger tips as she made sure all of the hair was wet. The whole experience was amazing: the soothing sensations of the shampoo as it was massaged in was invigorating; the joy as it was rinsed off as she knew it was about to be repeated all over again; the scent of the conditioner and the feeling of Shona combing it through to the tips of her hair topped the whole experience off and made her scalp tingle with an exciting sense of calm yet pleasure. Every touch sent a wave of pleasure straight through Kali.

"Oh my god, that was magical!"

"I'm glad you liked it."

Shona guided her back to the chair and massaged magnificently smelling serums and sprays into lengths of her hair before she started the blow-dry. She kept her eyes closed the whole time, the hum of the hair drier lulling her into such a relaxed state. When the treatment was finished, it took her a second or two to open her eyes. She felt and looked refreshed. The combination of the carbs, the coffee and the chill time worked absolute wonders and she felt like a new woman!

"Shona, I cannot believe that experience. It was truly   out   of   this   world!"

"Haha I am not going to lie, I thought I might need to wake you up at one point!" laughed Shona.

"Almost, you know me. I LOVE getting my hair done. But this time I truly experienced the whole thing.

I actually feel like I've had an hour of Reiki or a full body-massage!"

"Oh, I could really do with a wee massage myself! Haha! I'll tell you what, let's meet for a drink this week. As much as I loved having a silent session, I missed our chat! When are you free?"

With plans for Wine Wednesday made, she skipped to the car with a new found freshness. She jumped into her seat, flicked up her stories and went instantly live on her page.

"You won't believe it guys, just you wait 'til I tell you what I have just done!" she flicked her head to the side and brushed her hair forward. "I have just had the most AMAZING experience at my old faithful's, Blow and Glow." The smile was just beaming out from her, she just couldn't contain it. "As you all know, I went out with my mama yesterday and we may, or may not, have had just a few too many," she giggled. "I was feeling a little bit under the weather, and my bestie Shona offered me a silent treatment...A what?! I know!" she answered herself. "I had never heard of it either. But let me tell you, it is NEXT LEVEL! I felt every hair stroke, every sensation, every brush, and MY GOD it was amazing." She closed her eyes reliving the experience for just a second. "Honestly, try it! I will tag Blow and Glow in my caption, make a booking if you want to try it. You won't regret it!"

She chucked her phone on the passenger seat, took another look in the mirror and smiled at herself. That was two good deeds in one day. She turned on the ignition, checked her mirrors and headed straight home.

"Hugo!" she scooped her little pup as soon as she opened the door! "Oh, I missed you too, I missed you too!" she repeated as though he understood every word. She picked out her gilet from the coat rail and picked up his little harness and lead. "Let's go walkies!" as she put it on him, and they were both ready for a stroll through the park looking as chic and cool as ever.

She appreciated every moment as Hugo pranced through the leave covered paths. She smiled as she thought of how lucky she was. Only an hour and a half before Michael would be home, and they would be curled up with their favourite, but very rare treat of a take away. It also meant that there would be no dinner to prepare so she had plenty time to wander through the park. The simplest of things made her heart skip. *How could it honestly get any better than this?*

Chapter 17

Nicola

Nicola finally had to admit to herself, and to James, that the cleaner was a good idea. At first, she felt so betrayed by James; so inadequate and inferior. As though he thought she couldn't manage it all. But it was during one of her daily walks that she realised that she couldn't do it all. The help was actually just that, it was help, to make her life run smoother so that everything didn't depend on her. Help so that would enable her to live the life she wanted to.

Having a cleaner and getting the shopping delivered made life a little easier for her. Now that she had a little bit more of a routine in her life, she was able to put on a load of washing and hang it out each day or run around a room with a duster and hoover. If she didn't manage to get something done, she realised that it was ok, she was not as strict on herself with high expectations as she once was. This whole debacle has taught her that the world does not stop turning, in fact, quite the contrary, the world keeps turning, whether these things get done or not.

As much as she enjoyed exploring the wilderness around her city, she found that she enjoyed walking the streets too. As she crossed to the other side of town, she noticed that the houses got smaller and closer together. As she walked the neighbourhoods that were much livelier than her own, she seen families out on their bikes together, young mums walking with their prams, old friends meeting to walk their dogs. She noticed one thing that was common between all of them: they looked happy.

What was it that they had, that she didn't? She drove a fancier car and had a bigger house than they did. She had a husband and children who were all very successful in their own right. She had family that she kept in touch with and met weekly. But still she did not feel as happy as the strangers looked. As she continued on her walk, she thought about all of the things that made her truly happy. At that moment in time, the fresh air was all she could think of.

After walking for hours, she realised that she still wasn't any closer to figuring out why those other people looked so happy. She still couldn't figure out what made her properly, really and truly happy either. She realised that this wasn't right, as she had plenty of things that she *should* be happy about and decided to take the doctors recent advice and sign up for some counselling sessions as soon as she got home.

It was then, whilst walking back home through the park that she saw the parcel neighbour again. She remembered about how rude she was to her when she came to collect her parcel, and the heat rose up to her cheeks. The young woman was still walking towards her, with her little happy dog, both blissfully unaware of the potential awkward encounter. She felt as though she was trapped, there was nowhere else to go and nothing else to do but put her head down and keep walking. She glanced up to see if she noticed her, and was met with a friendly, welcoming smile. This threw her completely off, she was expecting some kind of drama, but instead, she was shown kindness. She lowered her head in shame and completed the final leg of her walk.

It was 4.30pm by the time Nicola got home. She went straight upstairs and searched her top drawer of her dresser and found the leaflet for the counselling sessions that Dr Rasheed had given her. She went online, filled out a referral form as quickly and impassively as she could, she did not want to feel any worse than she already did. She knew undergoing counselling sessions was a step in the right direction for her, and did not want to dwell on her unhappiness, and the happiness of others anymore.

She raided the fridge to see what she had available, and boiled up some pasta as she chopped up some veg. She made a simple tomato sauce and added it to the pasta and vegetables and topped it with cheese. She popped the dish in the oven to bake, along with a garlic baguette.

When dinner was ready, she set it out to cool and jumped into her car to pick the boys up from afterschool club. They were pleased yet shocked to see her since it was before closing time and the boys had gotten used to making their own way home now. Nicholas automatically gave her a big hug, while Jamie hovered at the back.

"Come on boys, let's go home before dinner gets cold."

The three of them hopped into the car and as they drove home, their mother asked them all about their days, as though the last month or so had never happened. The two boys shared bewildered glances at each other throughout the entire journey, whilst politely answering their mother's questions.

When they got home, they could smell the meal that their mother actually had indeed, prepared. Although they were taken aback, they were very grateful and had taken all that their mother had offered them. She had not had a proper conversation with them like this, in fact, they had not done anything remotely normal in a long time. But they did not question it, nor did they turn away from it. They simply enjoyed it for what it was, hoping that instances like this would happen more often and maybe eventually go back to normal.

When the meal was finished, the boys asked to be excused from the table, and instinctively fell into their usual routines. Jamie cleared away the plates and cutlery and loaded the dishwasher, whilst Nicholas wiped down the surfaces, tidied the kitchen, and swept the floors. Just like the old days.

While the boys were busy, she went into the cupboard and pulled out a board game that they used to always play when the boys were a little younger.

"Fancy a game?" she asked.

The boys looked at each other sceptically and shrugged their shoulders. "Why not?!"

The meal was eaten and cleared away, and board game in full swing all before 6pm. Normally, before life had changed, she would still be at work and wouldn't pick the boys up until 6 o'clock. Then it would be a mad rush to have dinner, get ready and get to their clubs in time for them starting. Tonight felt much less rushed, they had more time to spend together and do the things they enjoy.

It was then that Nicola realised that she had more fun with her boys tonight than she'd had in a long time. It embarrassed her to think that she couldn't even remember when the last time she'd actually had fun with them. And with that thought, she stood up, turned around, and walked straight up to her bedroom without another word. Leaving the boys at the table, not knowing what they had done wrong.

She spent the rest of the evening going between bouts of despair and sleeping. She didn't take the boys to their club as she promised. She had returned back to being the absent mother again.

Chapter 18

Emma

The countdown to the October holidays had dragged, but now it was finally here and Emma could not be more ready for it. After a long, hard week at work, Emma was exhausted. *That was some term,* as she thought over all that had happened in the space of just a short couple of months. The school did a complete 360 – from one of the most sought after schools in the area with a strong head teacher and the best manners and respect ever, to a school with behaviour problems and the head on sick leave, then back to a more positive school (head teacher still absent) and the behaviour was not quite where it used to be, but there was a definite improvement and still on the up. She was more relieved than ever to have 2 weeks off to spend at home with her family and kids.

She has known for some time that she needs to make amends with Dan. She hated the resentment that had built up between them over the past month. They used to be so good together. They used to *be* everything to each other. Them and their kids, nothing else mattered. Tonight, she decided, she was going to get it all back.

After work, she went to the supermarket and picked up pizzas, onion rings, crisps and sweets. It was more than she wanted to spend, but tonight was worth it. She put it on the credit card and decided to worry about it later. They'd been doing a lot of that lately. It was never big things, just £10 here and £20 there but she dreaded to think how much they'd spent, and how on earth they were going to be able to pay it back.

Emma planned a Millars family favourite night – a picnic in the middle of the living room with a movie. Normally Dan would push the sofas and furniture to the sides of the room and she would put down a big blanket and the 5 of them would sit on cushions and eat their tea on the floor. The lights would be dimmed, with candles on and fairy lights hanging from the door frame to the curtain pole. It was always so exciting, and even though Jasper was getting bigger, he still absolutely loved it.

But, because this was a surprise night, she rolled up her sleeves and pushed the sofas back with all of her might. It took much longer to set up as she was doing it alone, but they hadn't done it in such a long time and she knew that all of their faces would light up when they saw what she'd done for them. Even Dan's. And with that thought, a little smile spread across her face. She already felt better about their situation. They would kiss and make up and all would be well again.

Under the light of the twinkling fairy lights she admired her hard work, wiping off the sweat with the back of her hand. She opened the windows to let some fresh air in and gave the room a quick spritz of her favourite air freshener. *It wasn't perfect, but it was perfect for them,* she smiled and went through to put her shoes on to go collect the kids from school. It was just then, out of the corner of her eye she seen a piece of paper on the floor that she hadn't noticed when she came in earlier. She picked it up thinking it was an old receipt and went to put it in the bin when she recognised Dan's handwriting.

Her mouth fell open in disbelief as she read the note:

> *Emma,*
> *I have taken the kids to spend some time at my mums.*
>
> *We'll be back in a few days.*
>
> *Looks like we both have some thinking to do.*
> *Dan.*

Emma picked up her phone and called Dan to see what was going on. It was turned off. *Maybe it was an old letter,* she thought. But she racked her brains and couldn't ever remember a time when he went to his mums without her. She called him again. And again. And again. It just went straight to his answer machine every time. *Surely this must be some kind of mistake.*

She locked the door and headed to the school and for fear of being seen just in case, she stood further back than she normally would. She didn't want to speak to anyone, and she didn't want the teachers to see her just in case it was true. And right enough, the girls didn't come out of their usual gate. Every single child from the girls' class was dismissed to their parents and the teachers gladly shut the doors for the last time that term. All of Jasper's friends walked past round the corner but he was nowhere to be seen. She was glad she grabbed her sunglasses from the sideboard as she left; it was all she had to conceal the tears that welled up and silently fell from her eyes and rolled down her cheeks.

Emma doesn't even remember the walk home. She doesn't remember that she stepped on the road and a car had to swerve her as she tried to hurry past the school-run crowd. She didn't even notice as the girls' friends mum tried to speak to her. All she knew was that she needed to be home and when she got there, she went straight up to bed and shut the door before collapsing on her bed. Then she went back and opened it again so that she could hear when her family got home. She hoped that he was just doing this maybe to get her to think about things, and he'd only be gone a couple of hours.

The hours passed and there was no sign of her family. Emma tossed and turned trying to get comfy and drift off to sleep. But the thoughts that filled her head prevented that from happening. She had turned over the pillow's countless times. Sometimes, it was because her tears had saturated it and her face was sodden. The other times it was so that she could feel the cold side of the pillow on her swollen, red face. Neither provided relief for long.

The darkness was all consuming and Emma had never felt so alone. The bed felt huge without Dan there beside her. Normally he'd cuddle into her throughout the night. More often than not, she'd get too hot and roll away from him. Or lift his hand off of her. But now, more than ever she would give anything to feel his arm wrapped around her. Between the sobs of loneliness and thinking everything over in her head, she finally fell asleep.

When the sun started to rise and dimly light up the room through the gap in the curtains, she realised Dan still wasn't in bed with her. She checked the girls' and Jaspers rooms. Nope. Empty.

She started to walk downstairs and seen a light on from under the living room door. Her face lit up as she ran down the stairs, excited to see that her family were here after-all! He was only joking. Surely things couldn't be that serious after a few weeks of falling out! They had been married for years! Of course, things were fine! And the kids were here!

She burst through the door and looked on the sofa, and on to the picnic blanket on the floor, then to the front door, then to the sofa again. No one was there. The room was empty, except for the twinkling of the fairy lights that she'd set up the night before.

The realisation hit her and Emma fell to the sofa like the waves crashed into the cliffs on a stormy night. Dan and the kids really were gone.

Chapter 19

Kali

Kali rolled over and seen that Michael had finally joined her in bed. She had no idea what time he came home, but by 9pm she could no longer keep her eyes open. He had finally returned her text hours later, saying he has been busy and wouldn't be much longer. She had ordered his favourite food and waited on him to arrive. But he never did, and she ended up having to heat hers up in the microwave and eat it alone.

This was not the night she had planned at all. And now it was some time in the early hours of the morning and she was annoyed. She tried to roll over and go back to sleep, but she couldn't. She was annoyed that he wasn't there with her last night when she just wanted his cuddles. She was annoyed that she had hardly seen him at all over the last few weeks, and now she was annoyed that the great lump was snoring loudly in her ear. She turned round to face him and roll him over to face the other way. She pushed him a little harder than she probably should have, but she half wanted him to wake up too. If she couldn't sleep, then neither should he.

At some point in the night, she must have fallen back to sleep as Michael woke her up with a kiss. She was clearly still feeling bitter and shattered from being awake during the night for hours. She was absolutely not ready for his pleasantries, especially considering he had not even apologised to her yet. She didn't even acknowledge him and just rolled over.

"Wake up sleepy head" he tickled her arm playfully.

"You've got to be joking me!" she grumbled.

"Come on, Kali. I have hardly seen you!" he rolled her over to look in her eyes which weren't even open yet.

"Michael, I didn't even get to see you yesterday. Not once. You sneaked away in the morning, I hardly heard from you all day, you missed dinner, and you came home when I was already asleep! So don't roll me over and tell me you've hardly seen me. I've been right here. Where were you!?"

"Sorry babe, I was just busy, that's all" he said as he kissed her arm.

She pulled her arm away and sat bolt upright. "Michael, I feel like I haven't seen you for weeks." Worries she didn't even know she had rose from deep in her subconscious and straight out of her mouth.

"I know, I have just been so busy, you know how it is" he pleaded with her.

"I am busy too, you know, but I always make time for you," a tear rolled down her face which shocked the two of them.

"Why are you crying, what are you saying?!"

Kali turned round, lay back down with her back towards him. "Go have your shower and go to work, Michael."

He tried to speak to her, but she was having none of it. Guiltily, he done as he was told and went into the shower so as not to upset her any more.

It wasn't like her to be so grumpy with Michael, she just wasn't a grumpy person by nature. When he finally left to go to work, she went downstairs and made her hot ginger and lemon and sipped on it as she made her smoothie. She went outside with her yoga mat and worked her way through her routine, calming herself and thinking rationally again. As she progressed through her routine, her thoughts became more logical and she had found herself acting like she was someone else, that it wasn't her and Michael having this argument. She did not like it one bit. She reminded herself that he is in a crucial part of his career and he really is working hard to boost it as much as he can and that she should be a little bit more understanding and less selfish about the situation.

At peace with herself again, she felt ready and able to start ticking off items on her list for the day. First up, was a toaster clean. She had noticed when she made her bagel the other day that it was full of crumbs and could do with a wee wipe down. She set up her tripod and placed her phone at the perfect angle to ensure that she'd get a full shot of the toaster as well as her face. She emptied out the contents of the drawer onto the worktop and tipped the toaster upside down, adding that to the pile too. "I am sure everyone's toaster is just like mines – don't forget to include it in your monthly cleans like I did!" knowing to make her content more relatable, not letting on that she, in fact, has a cleaner and doesn't often need to clean anything other than for creating content for her page.

Also on the agenda today was "outfit inspo" content for a brand she had promoted a few times before. This time, it was for their new Autumn Winter collection; ribbed gym leggings complete with a phone thigh pocket and a matching oversized hoody. Kali loved them. Not that she ever wore them going to the gym of course! She just loved how comfortable and cosy they were just for every day wear. She tried on all 4 sets that was sent to her, the same outfit, the same sizes, just in a variety of nude tones. She filmed herself as she did, posing in between each with a variety of head tilts and foot-kicks. She edited the clips into a 30 second reel and posted it with her discount code and the link to purchase the items with 10% off.

She kept on the final outfit - a little khaki green number. It was a little more colour than she was used to wearing, but she loved how it went with her white sports socks and cream Crocs, paired with her faithful mac jacket. Perfect for walking the dog! And with that thought, she pulled out Hugo's little khaki quilted coat and popped it on him. She loved to match with him! She posed for a picture and sent it to Michael with the caption "matchy-matchy!" before they set off on a wee jaunt around the block.

She also used the opportunity to share little Hugo with her followers, they loved seeing what he was up to. She filmed her feet walking with the leaves on the ground and slowly panned the camera up towards him as he pranced along, and as she called his name out, he stopped and turned towards the camera, tilting his head as Pomeranians so often do. *Perfect* smiled Kali, as she uploaded the video to her story. *They would go wild for that one!*

The final piece of work for the day was yesterday's cancelled content for Cuisine. Her deadline for the content was a week on Friday, but she liked to work fast. The quicker she got her work done, the quicker she could do something else. But, of course, she did not compromise on quality in favour of speed. Oh no. It was quality every time for her. She was just super organised and efficient, and she reaped what she sowed in terms of quality and hard work.

On tonight's Cuisine menu was a simple dish of pea and ham risotto. Just like every other time she promoted content for this brand, she videoed herself making the meal from scratch. After she had eaten, she would edit it ready to post for inspiration around 3pm tomorrow. That way, when people were starting to think about what they were going to have for dinner, they might be hungry enough and inspired to try Cuisine, and then she would earn more endorsements from it than she would if she posted it after dinner time. It was all about the timing, maximising the chances of a click or a purchase from a link, and she knew exactly how to get the biggest bang for her buck!

Dinner was ready and sitting in the pot waiting for Michael to arrive home. He should have been back by now, so she called him but there was no answer. Trying not to feel annoyed, she reminded herself of her realisation during her yoga earlier and sent him a message asking him to let her know when he was on his way so that she could plate up dinner. She decided to clean up while she waited, popped all of the dishes into the dishwasher and wiped down all of the worktops. She was hungry by now, so much so that she was starting to feel a little bit sick. A whole hour had passed since her last text and yet there was still no reply. Nothing even from the matchy-matchy message earlier. She decided to heat up her dinner and eat alone again, for the second night in a row.

Chapter 20

Nicola

Stepping into the counsellor's office was a huge step for Nicola. Massive. She was a woman who did not like to get things wrong, never mind admit them when she did. For her, attending therapy was an admission that she didn't get things right.

At her first session Nicola was asked to share why she found herself at therapy. She explained that everything in life was going well, she was successful, busy and efficient at both home and school. But after things started to go wrong at home, she found that everything began to crumble around her and she could no longer cope with the strains and pressures that life threw at her. She explained that she had been on medication for around 6 weeks, and although now she had begun to get some structure back into her life, she found it difficult to feel happy, despite everything else that she had. She shared how, when out for a walk she seen several people who may not have been as career driven or as financially successful, but that they seemed happier than she was, and it bothered her. That was the final straw for her, her reason why she finally decided to try therapy.

The counsellor asked her if she thought that having more things made her better than other people.

Without even needing to think about it she answered, "of course not."

"So why do you place such emphasis on happiness in relation to what you have?" Nicola thought about it for a moment and disagreed.

"It's not that I think that having more things makes you happy. It's more the point that I have so many things to be happy about, that I can't understand why I don't feel happy."

Through their conversation, she had not realised that she had been subconsciously thinking that having more meant you would be happier. She was mortified. They explored where this belief system she had unknowingly developed came from and explored the reasons. It could be, that as a head teacher, Nicola knew that the more deprived one is, the more difficulty they are likely to face in life. But she also knew that this wasn't a fail-safe theory, there was always, and will always be multiple instances where this wasn't the case. She then thought about how it could perhaps be a result of how she was brought up. Maybe, but she had a happy childhood, her parents spent lots of time loving and caring for her and her siblings that there was no stone there she could uncover.

She then thought of the parcel woman she seen at the park, her final straw for attending therapy, and realised indeed that it is not in fact what you have, or how powerful or successful you are that makes you happy. This girl was young, pretty, and had her whole life ahead of her. And even when people were mean to her, happiness still shone out of her like sunbeams. Yet, she was aware of all of the power and success that she had, more than one could ever need, but still she felt overwhelmingly sad and out of control.

As her therapist helped her work though her emotions, she was given the homework of "accepting it as it is, and to grow and heal from it." Just because it was something she had been subconsciously trained to think, it doesn't need to be the way she continues to think. The therapist then said something which really shook her.

"You should always treat people the way you want to be treated."

This was something she preached, day in day out at school. With her staff, and with her pupils. And here she was, feeling like she was being told off for not doing that very thing.

When the tears formed in her eyes the therapist encouraged her to let it all out. She said how she felt like she had been a fraud, giving out advice and living life like she was this amazing thing. When in fact, she did not even know who she was or what made her truly happy.

That night in bed, she lay thinking about all of the times she had treated people differently for what they had, or what their social status was. The cleaners, the bin men, the dinner ladies, her neighbours, her staff, her family. She thought of the fear she had seen in people's faces as they wondered whether or not she would be pleased with them. This was not the type of person that Nicola wanted to be. It was not the type of person that she was, deep down.

The next day, after a good night's sleep, she thought of how she could work on changing and perhaps develop new habits. Not placing emphasis on the having things, but actually on *enjoying* things. With her homework in mind, she set herself a goal; she was going to try not to judge others, to take them as they presented themselves to her.

She also knew that over time, she wanted to right the wrongs that she had done. Not that she had ever done anything that bad to anyone, but it hurt her to know that she had without malice hurt or caused fear in people, and she wanted to make it up to them.

Chapter 21

Kali

Kali sat herself down in the salon ready for Carly to help her decide what nail colour to go for.

"Oh, I have honestly tried to think of something, I have spent ages looking online…," said Kali. "Maybe a nice nude colour, or maybe just a classic French? Oh, I don't know!"

"Well, you have had block colours for the past few visits, and I do know you love to return to your old favourite French!" Carly admitted. "Hang on, I actually have one you might love" and she opened her drawer and pulled out a brownie-nude with just a hint of lilac.

"Oh, that is so nice!" Kali tilted the bottle to examine the different shades of the bottle in the light. "It's called 'Modern Love!'"

"Oh, I am not sure if that's what you'd call it?!" said Kali, not even realising what was coming out of her mouth.

"What do you mean?"

The two girls spent the next hour dissecting her life. She explained how for the past few weeks she hadn't seen Michael almost at all, and when she did, she found herself being snappy with him. She said how she had been out drinking twice in one week, and how

Wine Wednesday ended up messier than she planned and that she was still hungover from it. She had planned on just sharing a bottle with Shona, but one bottle turned into two, then into three. She woke up in the morning not remembering much of the night at all, or how she even got home. She had a banging headache and couldn't stop being sick all day. Even this morning she woke up and was still feeling sick.

At that moment, the blood drained from her face and the nausea crept up as she reached for the bucket and vomited right into it

"Oh Carly, my god, I am so sorry…" said Kali, looking at the mess in embarrassment.

"Are you ok?"

"My god, I have never ever been this sick with the drink…," It was with a stark realisation that Kali counted back the days and realised that her period was almost a week late. The blood drained from her face and she turned a grey shade of green. "Oh God, I think I am pregnant."

The two girls sat mouths ajar in stunned silence.

"That would explain the nausea, the hunger and mood swings I've been having…" she muttered, her eyes searching the ceiling as if it held all the answers fizzing around in her brain.

"Ok, that's great news, is it not?!" asked Carly hopefully, as she put the bucket in the back to deal with later.

"I don't know! We have never even spoke about it properly before. And if we had, it certainly wouldn't be on the radar any time soon…And he's been so distant recently. I am not even sure if he wants me anymore, never mind a baby!" The nausea was still there, threatening to erupt again. And the thought of losing Michael made it ten times worse.

Kali wasn't paying attention to what was going on around her. Her nails were finished, but she couldn't think of anything other than the thought of maybe being pregnant, and her envisioned face of Michael as she broke the news to him.

She made Carly swear not to tell a single soul and drove home via the pharmacy to pick up a pregnancy test. She decided there was no point telling anyone, especially Michael, until she found out if she was actually pregnant or not.

£18 for a two pack of the highest quality tests later, she found herself driving home in absolute turmoil. *My God, what would she do if she were pregnant? What would Michael do? Would they even be together anymore? How could everything go from being perfect to this in such a short space of time?*

She parked in the drive, unlocked her front door and didn't even acknowledge Hugo as she went straight upstairs to her ensuite. There were several toilets in the house, but if she was going to find out she was pregnant, she was going to find out in the one she felt most comfortable in – her ensuite.

She sat on the toilet seat lid and opened the box carefully to read the instructions. She steadied herself on the side and braced herself physically and emotionally for what was about to happen. She lifted the lid, pulled down her bottoms and pants and readied the test in her hand as she sat down on the toilet seat, ready to pee on the stick for the stated 5 seconds. Just as she was about to start the stream, she noticed that there was blood all over her pants. Her period had arrived.

She spent the rest of the afternoon, curled up on the sofa watching films with a hot water bottle soothing her tummy cramps. She had never cried so much. Two films in, and Hugo was pestering her: barking and pawing at her, desperate for his walk.

Reluctantly, she pulled on a pair of trainers, her coat and set off down the park. She had zero motivation to walk at all, and so found an empty bench and just sat there staring into the bright blue autumnal sky as Hugo frolicked around her on the lead extension. She thought of all that she had, and all that she didn't. She wasn't even sure if she wanted the baby, but now the choice was taken away from her, she felt sad and empty. And lonely. Again.

A sound of laughter in the distance caught her attention, and she found herself drawn to a family playing frisbee. She couldn't make out what they found so funny, but two young girls were giggling cheeky, mischievous little laughs, bouncing off each other and laughing louder and louder. She noticed the look on their parents faces as they watched their girls. She sat watching the family for some time, she wasn't sure exactly how long. But their game had finished and they all walked off into the sunset together. Two adults, a son and two beautiful, giggly girls.

She cried then and there, in the middle of the park. Not aware or even caring if anyone was watching her.

She realised exactly what she wanted. Kali wanted a family.

Without waiting for Michael to come home any longer, she went upstairs and poured herself a large glass of wine, ran a bath and lit a candle.

Instagram: #whisperingangel #espabath #metime. Reality: sobbing in the bath, knocking back the wine, never felt worse.

Chapter 22

Nicola

At her next therapy session, Nicola was asked to bring up the reasons why she thought everything came crashing down around her. She recalls the point, clearly, when she received a phone call from her son's school about his behaviour. She relived the same emotions then as she did on the day. The shock and disbelief, the anger, the disappointment, and the embarrassment. The therapist helped her talk through each of her emotions, and she soon realised that the embarrassment was the one that affected her the most; the thought of what others thought of her son, and by proxy, what they thought of her.

She had never been the type of person who she thought would care about what others thought. She done everything because she thought it was how it should be done, and because she wanted to do it. But here she was, sitting in someone else's office that she barely knew, realising that she done everything to please others. Not anyone in particular, per se. But in just people pleasing everyone in general. She thought that by being the best she could be, no one could ever want, or indeed ask any more of her. But it was all just a show. The house, the cars, the private school for her kids and all of the extra-curricular activities she arranged for them. Yes, she enjoyed having all of these things, but did she actually *enjoy* them? Did they improve her life at all? Did she take the time to appreciate them for what they are? Did she take the time to enjoy her family?

She dug deep literally and physically, she clenched her firsts and pushed her hands as far down into her pockets as she could, took a deep breath, and shared her biggest embarrassment. The thing that hurt her the most. Nicola felt like she didn't even know her own children. Something so big and so bad was going on inside her boys and she didn't know about it until it was too late. And now, here she is, with a family she can't even spend any time with without an all-consuming sense of guilt.

She described how she tried to spend time with the boys over the last few weeks, but doing so only made her feel worse. When she cooked them dinner for the first time in a long time, she was impressed with how mature and grown up the boys had been. She pulled out a board game and she actually laughed and enjoyed their company. Then her head suddenly filled with dark clouds as she couldn't think of one single time in the last 5 years when she actually sat down and played with them. Her heart broke in two as she re-lived the moment.

She then told of the several other similar instances that had occurred, like the time when she asked the boys to go out for a walk with her. They went, but they didn't enjoy the walk and simply moaned about when they would be back home. She was upset that they didn't share her enjoyment or even at least appreciate the fresh air like she did, or that they didn't even seem to enjoy her company. And then, just last week when she went to get the boys early from afterschool club but they weren't finished their homework yet, so they said they would just walk home when they were ready. She described how rejected she felt, and how after that incident she made no further effort to engage with her sons.

Through their conversation, she realised that no matter how mature they seemed, and were actually more than capable of looking after themselves, they were still, indeed, children. She had over the recent years viewed them as big boys, focusing solely on their academic achievements and their career-paths that she forgot that they were actually still very young.

And in terms of the rejection and disengagement she felt from them, both of these emotions were perfectly normal. From the boys' point of view, they hadn't spent any time with their mother for some time and suddenly, she was asking them to give up their only free time in their busy schedule to go out for a walk. They went to appease her, but they are still only 12 and 13 and had probably been looking forward to playing on their consoles and talking to their friends online all week. It's not that they didn't miss or want to spend any time with their mum at all, it's just that they had other expectations for the evening.

The incident where she went to pick them up from afterschool club early, the therapist suggested that perhaps the boys weren't rejecting her. They were focused on their studies as she had raised them to be, and they simply wanted to finish their work before they came home, the same way they always had done. It was their routine.

Nicola finally started to see things from Jamie and Nicholas' point of view. None of these instances meant that they didn't want to spend time with their mother, she had no reason to be feeling rejected.

She thought of her long term goal of fixing things and decided that she would start with building up her time with her sons to try to get to know the real them; what they want from life, and who they are. Not just what Nicola wants them to have from life, and who she wants them to be.

That evening whilst the boys were at afterschool club, Nicola had prepared the boys' favourite meals from when they were little. It was a simple Spaghetti Bolognese that her own mother taught her to make. The rich, garlicky smell was nostalgic, it brought her back to her mother's kitchen when she was little. Then it zoomed her back to their old kitchen in the semi, with the two matching high chairs and two hungry, excited boys were squealing for their favourite.

It wasn't often that Nicola looked back on life. She was a fast-paced, career driven woman who always looked forward. But recently she found she was doing it more and more often. She wasn't sure if it was the medication, the therapy, the extra time she had, or the fact that she was beginning to heal. But she soon realised that looking back wasn't a bad thing. It helped her remember who she was, and where she came from. It also meant that she could treasure moments that were important to her.

The boys came bursting through the door, laughing at each other, not expecting to see their mother in the kitchen with dinner laid on the dining table. They looked at each other, and back to their mother with their real smiles fading. They quickly replaced their expression with a replica smile.

"Look, I know things have been hard for you boys. But I want you to know, I am trying."

"I know mum, I am sorry" replied Nicholas.

"Sorry for what, darling? I am the one who has been absent here."

Nicholas glanced at Jamie, and then back down to his plate.

"I promise, I am trying to get better."

Sitting at the head of the table, she reached out and put her hand on top of each of the boys.'

They spent the rest of the evening cosied up on the sofa, watching a film together. There was no phones, no conversations, just a mum and her two sons laughing at a comedy. She put the replica smile to the back of her mind, and tried to remember that they were just still children. She pulled them both close, gave them a kiss on their heads and snuggled in. The rest of the night was perfect. The best night she could ever think of.

At her next session, Nicola brought up the replica smile to her therapist. She was dreading the conversation, as it confirmed to her just how much the boys didn't want to spend time with her. Especially after feeling so good about the sofa cuddles with her boys, it was just what she needed. What they all needed. But the therapist explored the possibility of it being quite the contrary: the fact that she even *knew* that it was a replica smile meant that she did know the boys better than she thought. She could tell when they were genuine in their emotions or not. Furthermore, it also meant that the boys cared about her. They were so intent on making their mother happy, that perhaps they faked their emotions to conceal their worry. A very mature response for them to have at such a young age.

A sense of relief washed over her. She wasn't used to over thinking everything she, or others done. But the therapist warned that we don't want to get in the habit of over-thinking, but just learning to see things as they are.

"Appreciate them for all that they are and grow and heal" - know that things don't stay the same forever.

Chapter 23

It was while she was out on her walk one day that Nicola realised how kind, thoughtful, and responsible her boys really were. She knew that she had given them all of the skills and abilities needed to do well in life. She didn't want to force them into being anything that they weren't. She knew only too well how life turned out when you masked everything just to make it look good.

Over the next few weeks, the time she spent with the boys increased significantly. She spent time getting to know them, finding about their friends. Learning what their favourite music was, their favourite video games, and what books they liked to read. She felt so much more relaxed around them now that the academic pressure was off and she tried so hard to make up for lost time and enjoy what was left of their childhood with them.

As she began to relax and open up to her boys, they, in turn, did the same. They started speaking about the future and what they wanted to be when the grow up. Nicholas told her that it had always been his dream to join the RAF just like his dad, and his grandad before him. Nicola had no idea. She always pictured him to be a doctor or a dentist. But now he had said it, she realised that it was the perfect career for him. He was naturally good at following orders from above and passing them on down below. He shared his desire to see the whole world, to live his life to fullest and progress in his career and be successful just like his dad. She smiled to herself, imagining him standing to attention in his uniform, and swallowed the lump in her throat as she realised that it could potentially only be another 4 years before he could join up.

Jamie declared that he didn't know what he wanted to do when he was older yet, and bashfully played with the lining of his hoodie.

"Jamie, you can tell me." She reassured him, squeezing him into her a little tighter.

He trusted her, knowing that his old mum would have laughed at him for having such an idea. But his new mum, she seemed much more open and relaxed. He gambled and decided to tell her anyway.

"I… I have always wanted to be a computer game developer, mum." He couldn't lift his eyes up for fear of her response.

"Oh, have you now?!" she teased, tickling him between his neck and collarbone.

"Do you think I paid all of that money on your education just for you to play video games all day?!" she picked up the pillow and whacked it over his head. He was in shock, but as he looked up, he saw she had the biggest smile. Jamie picked up his pillow and hit his mum right over the head unexpectedly and she went flying over onto the bed. The three of them erupted into laughter and had a massive, full-on pillow fight. She climbed on top of Nicholas to get him back and was whacking him over the face with her pillow, while Jamie started whacking her over the back of the head until she clambered off of Nicholas, then the two of them ganged up on their mum. It was something they had never done before, and Nicola didn't know where the idea came from, but she was glad she had it. The boys were loving this new, playful side of their mother they had never experienced before.

As they lay on the bed in exhausted joy, Jamie reached over and pulled out his sketch book. "Can I show you something, Mum?"

"Of course, what is it?" she asked as she sat up and got herself comfy.

He sat back down next to her and opened up his book. The colour and detail he had drawn was breath-taking.

"I have been designing this one for ages. It's a time-travel game, where you can build and create your own worlds in different time dimensions."

Nicola was amazed that her son had created something so wonderful, something so amazing. She did not know he even liked drawing, never mind that he had the ability to produce something like this.

As he flicked through the pages, describing the different possibilities in each of the worlds, Nicola couldn't wipe the smile from her face. Pride poured out of every pore.

"Mum, what's wrong?" Nicholas wiped a tear from her face before she realised that she was crying.

"Oh boys! I am just so happy for the both of you. How well you have done, considering everything…"

Jamie suddenly threw himself into his mum's arms and cried hysterically. Big, fat sobs were wailing out of him. She wasn't sure if he couldn't speak, or wouldn't speak to her, so Nicola pulled him onto her knee and cuddled into him stroking his hair like she used to when he was little. Nicholas put his hand on his mum's knee. He didn't know what else do to, but he knew that he wanted to be there for the both of them. The first time he left his mother and brother sobbing haunted him still to this day. He felt he let himself, and his family down. And that he was the reason that things weren't getting any better – because he couldn't step up to the plate.

When Jamie eventually settled into his mother's soothing ways, he finally began to open up.

"I am so sorry I made you sick, Mum." It was barely a whisper.

"What? No honey, you didn't make me sick. This is nothing to do with you. I was trying to do too much, to be perfect at everything, and I couldn't cope. It all just came crashing down."

"It's all my fault!" he wailed, reaching further into his mum for comfort.

"Jamie, look at me," she grabbed his face and looked straight into his eyes. "This wasn't you. None of this. It was me! It's all my fault, I never took the time to really get to know you." she squeezed her hand tighter into Jamie's. "To get to know both of you. And I am so, so sorry. You will never know how sorry I am. But I promise I will spend every day from now on making it up to you. I just want you to know, that everything I have ever done, I have done out of my best intentions for you. I only ever wanted the best for you." She kissed both of her boys on their heads.

"The only difference is now I realise that what is best for you is not necessarily what I think is right for you."

She nudged Jamie off of her, ruffled his hair and took a step back to look at the both of them. "And here I was having the both of you a doctor and a lawyer!" as she pointed to each of her boys with her envisioned professions.

Jamie laughed "A lawyer?! You have got to be kidding me!"

"Ah Jamie, you have always been the feistier one. You could argue your way out of anything!"

That night she called James for a chat to share the news of her night with the boys. He was so surprised to see his phone light up with her picture on the screen as over recent times it was always him who had to initiate contact. He could feel the subtle change in her, his old Nicola was coming back to him. He could not wait to get home tomorrow night, which was also something new in recent times. He hated coming home and seeing how much she had deteriorated in just the space of a couple of months.

That night, Nicola had never felt closer to her boys and went to bed wearing a smile.

Chapter 24

Nicola's self-care routine was now well established with her daily walks and getting back to nature. Strolling through the streets or exploring the local country side, it didn't matter. Just being out in the fresh air made all the difference to her mood. A walk in the morning really cleared her mind and set her up for the day. She used the time to visualise how her day would go, what she would do and the experiences she would have. She also used the time to think about things that had gone well the day before, and what things she wanted to improve. She really listened to her inner voice, and now focused on becoming a better person, rather than the person she thought she needed to be. She was proud of how far she'd come in such a short space of time.

But not only was she looking after herself better, finally her home-life seemed to be back in order too. The house was clean and tidy, with the added help of their cleaner. The fridge and cupboards were stocked up with provisions, and the freezer was back to being full of batch home-cooked meals. She and her family were enjoying more time together.

Friday night became Family night. The 4 of them shared a meal and played board games. The boys stayed up later than they normally got to so that they could all watch a film together. It became something to look forward to for each of them. The boys didn't mind giving up their free-time Friday because they now had a whole Monday night to themselves since they, as a family, decided to give up swimming. The boys had passed all of their swimming qualifications and had the certificates to prove it. It was only a requirement of their mothers for them to attend swimming lessons to ensure that they would be safe whenever they went near water. But now they were proficient in life-saving skills, it was agreed that they could maybe stop the swimming lessons since they didn't particularly enjoy them anymore anyway.

The thing was, now that Mondays were free, the boys actually went out to play with the other boys on the street. One night they were sitting in their rooms playing their PS5s when Jamie heard noise coming from outside. He looked out of his window and seen that there were some kids out in the street were playing football. Jamie couldn't recall ever seeing anyone out playing in the street before, so he ran through to his brother's room and threw a pair of goalie gloves at him. "Fancy a game?!"

The two boys now had the time from the change to their busy schedule and found that they now had the energy to physically socialise. It was good for them, to just go out and have a kick about with their friends for fun, rather than just doing activities because they had to. Nicola enjoyed watching them out the window playing whilst she washed the dishes. She laughed to herself as she wondered if the only reason that they went out to play was because their mother let them off with their chores that night.

The final item on Nicola's fix it list, was work. There was only a couple of weeks left until the end of term, so she wanted to dedicate some time to building herself back up to be able to return back to work after the October holidays. Through her therapy sessions she realised that the way she was working was not sustainable. She was working at least 12 hours a day 5 days a week at work, and then all of the time she was working at home on top of that. She was actually working more than double the contracted hours per week. And this wasn't just on one-off, special or busy weeks such as the lead up to parents evening, or Christmas. This was every single working week of the year. Other than it not being sustainable and detrimental to her mental health and wellbeing, she just simply wasn't paid enough for the hours she put in. Later, when she calculated it, the salary she received for the hours she worked was actually laughable. But it really helped put things into perspective. For her average hourly rate, she would be as well ditching all of the responsibility and finding a job stacking the shelves in her local supermarket, and this was with a decent head teacher wage!

She also thought about her staff whom she knew also worked long, unsustainable hours. She made it her mission to explore different ways to help improve the work-life balance for herself, and every staff member within her school.

She scoured the internet for research papers on teacher work-life balance and spent the next week drafting up reports and plans to present to her SLT. Normally when Nicola wanted to make changes, she just done it without consulting anyone because she knew best. But that was not how she wanted to run things anymore. The changes she was proposing would cause a drastic change to the workplace and Nicola wanted to make sure everyone was on board before she implemented them.

Finally, when she was happy with her plans, she made up a PowerPoint and flipchart poster to present to her staff. Nicola had done this hundreds of times, it was her bread and butter. But this time, she felt nervous. Nervous for the suggested changes, nervous to actually stand up and deliver her presentation. But this was something she knew she had to do. Not just for herself, but for her staff too.

James sat back and watched his wife slowly morph back into the woman she was before. Although, this time she wasn't quite the same. She was a strong and independent woman before, but now she was a strong and independent woman with a cause to fight for, and he couldn't be prouder. Without wanting to distract her, he just continued to sit in his arm chair by the window, sipping on his cup of tea admiring the woman he had loved for all of those years, and whom he loved now more than ever before.

She picked up the phone and dialled her office with bated breath. Jackie answered the phone and was surprised to hear her boss on the line. But not just because she was calling her, but because of her tone and how she actually was on the other end of the phone. She seemed...different.

Jackie shared the news with Donna that Nicola would be in on Friday to deliver a presentation at their SLT meeting. That was in just two days' time. They had a lot to do before their boss returned to work. It was all hands on deck to make sure that everything was running exactly as she liked it. There was to be no emails left unanswered, no coats or bags left hanging on pegs in the corridors, and the manners of the children had to be beyond excellent. They did not want to let Nicola down and let her think that they'd been slacking whilst she'd been off.

When Friday arrived, Jackie and Donna could not believe how fast the last two days had flown. For Nicola, on the other hand, it was a different story. Although she was extremely nervous, she just couldn't wait to get back in there and make some positive changes.

She arrived early, with a tray of coffees for her SLT hoping for a catch up before her presentation. They were not prepared for it at all, and they waffled their way through the conversation.

"Let's have a look for ourselves, eh?" Nicola stood up, picked up her bag. Jackie and Donna shared a glance at each other. "Well, come on then?!"

As they walked through the school, children greeted her as though she had never left.

"Good morning, Mrs Smythe," came a small voice from a girl who held the door open for the SLT to walk through.

"Good morning, Emily," Nicola smiled back.

The school was spotless. Nicola popped into each class, the behaviour seemed good, and the children's manners were still there. There was still one important place to visit – the staff room at lunch time. This would reveal the truth to her about how things were whilst she was gone. And she started to suddenly feel more nervous about this than her presentation.

Just then, the bell rang to signal lunch, and Nicola made her way straight to the staffroom. She boiled the kettle and brought out a box of fancy biscuits from her bag, the kind that only usually came out at Christmas. As the staff filtered in, they seemed happier than ever to see her.

"How are you?"

"How have you been?"

"Are you feeling better now?"

"Oh, we have missed you!"

The concerns and worry from her staff was reassuring. She spent 20 minutes chatting to everyone and let them all know that she was looking forward to coming back after the school holidays.

"Remember to take time out and look after yourselves. Rest, you know next term is always crazy with the Christmas shows to prep for and the general excitement of everyone!"

She went through to the conference room to set up for her presentation to her SLT. She went over the PowerPoint one last time, before she finally felt ready to deliver it.

She spent the rest of the time looking out of the window watching the children of her school running round and playing. She realised that the school didn't stop functioning just because she was off sick. In fact, it seemed to be running rather well without her. She then worried that the presentation would not land as well as she initially thought it would.

Just then, Jackie and Donna arrived with their notepads and took a seat.

"First of all, I just wanted to say there are a few things I noticed as soon as I arrived."

Jackie and Donna were so nervous, it was clearly visible on their faces.

"The first thing I noticed was there was still a positive atmosphere in the school. The children all still expressed good manners, and everyone seems so supportive of each other. And of me. So, thank you. From the bottom of my heart, thank you for all you have done and continue to do for me."

The tension in the room lifted in an instant. The SLT did not know what to expect when their leader returned. They were worried about the backlash of not doing things the way she had wanted them done. But there was no mention of that at all, nothing but praise and gratitude.

When the presentation was finished, both women stood up and clapped a round of applause. Nicola was gob-smacked. She thought it was good, but she had no idea if it would be received well at all.

"Nicola, you have to share this with the staff before they come off for the holidays." Stated Jackie.

Donna chipped in "Absolutely, we can get to work on it right away, there's no time like the present!"

"What a great idea, I think we should share it. But

weren't you listening to me? The whole point of this is to reduce workload. So no, I am not going to have you working through the holidays just to get it up and running. That kind of defeats the whole purpose!" Nicola laughed. She was grateful for their suggestions, but this was not the way to achieve it.

"Nicola, when have we ever NOT worked in the holidays? Come on, it will be better if we get it all up and running at the start of the term." said Jackie convincingly.

Donna chipped in again, "Start the way we mean to go on, eh?!"

After sharing her new ideas with the rest of the teaching staff. They had agreed to all of her ideas, and the new improvement plan was going to be underway very soon.

Arrangements were made with her SLT to get together during the holidays and sort out the ideas and get them into fruition. But the only way Nicola agreed to this, was with the promise of a party at her house afterwards. But by the time this was arranged, most of the rest of the staff were gone. Nicola sat at her desk, feeling happy to finally be back there. She went through all of her colleagues details and took note of their phone numbers with the intention of inviting them, along with her friends and family to a BBQ in the holidays. This was going to be some party, and she couldn't wait!

Nicola left the school feeling extremely elated. A stark contrast from how she was feeling the last time she left school, just 6 weeks before.

As she pulled up into her drive, Nicola caught sight of the parcel-woman neighbour's house and decided to give the door a chap to invite her round to the BBQ too. She wanted to fix things and didn't want any negativity between them, and she really truly was sorry for her behaviour towards her. She also felt drawn to her, because it was seeing her that was the realisation that perhaps she did need a little help with some counselling after all. Not that the parcel neighbour knew anything about any of that, but Nicola wanted to make it up to her.

She rang the doorbell and waited. No one answered. She turned around and headed straight into her empty house. May as well get the ball rolling, she thought. She turned on her computer and made a massive home shopping order for the BBQ. She had no idea how many people would turn up, but she ordered enough food and drink to feed a small army.

With her little fix-it list almost pretty much completed; Nicola felt the need to celebrate. She called her husband to see how far away he was. He was half an hour away and the boys wouldn't be home for another hour yet. She jumped in the shower to freshen up and dressed ready to go out for dinner and drinks instead of their usual family Friday night. When James got home, Nicola had the glint in her eye again that he'd all but forgotten about.

"There she is!" James swept Nicola up and carried her upstairs like he had when they first got together.

Chapter 25

Emma

Emma was woken up in the afternoon with her phone vibrating. She sat bolt up-right and her hand scurried around blindly until she found her phone. She closed her eyes, wiped the slumber-slavers from her cheek and drew in a deep breath and braced herself to hear from Dan. She unlocked her phone and it was a message from an unknown number.

> *Hi, I hope you are enjoying*
> *the start of your October break.*
> *I am having a BBQ next Saturday*
> *Afternoon and would be most*
> *grateful if you could attend.*
> *Look forward to seeing you,*
> *Nicola Smythe.*

Emma was in utter disbelief. A message from her Head Teacher. *Is she kidding me? Why would I ever choose to spend time, my own personal time, with her?* Emma couldn't wait to be off for a fortnight, no way was she going to spend any of it with the one person at work who made her feel worthless. In anger, she threw her phone across the room.

And with that thought, a deep, guttural sound came from the pit of her stomach. She really did feel worthless now. A husband who had left her and taken her kids: her only reason for being. Everything she done was for her family, and now she found herself with nothing. She crawled along the picnic blanket and reached for her phone, desperate now more than ever to hear from her husband and speak to her kids. She dialled Dan's number and again, it just went straight to his answering machine.

It had been almost 24 hours since Emma had found that note. And numerous calls to his number, none of them even ringing through once. As much as it pained her, she called her mother in laws landline. She just had to know they were ok.

"Hello, Debbie? It's Emma…Yes, I am ok. I just wanted to check if Dan and the kids were with you?... Ah ok, do you know when he'll be back?... Ok. Please tell him that I called."

Once again, the silent tears were rolling down Emma's cheeks. At least she knew now that Dan and the kids were definitely there. They were safe. That is the only silver lining that she was able to salvage from the awful fact that her family had deserted her.

In a sudden wave of motivation, Emma moved all of the furniture back to their original position and not a trace of the planned happy family picnic night remained. She sat down on her armchair and pulled out her phone and began scrolling through her feed. She came across a post where a room had been renovated on a budget and it gave her an idea. Dan and the kids were away, she had tried to contact him and now that he knew she was looking for him, she could do nothing else but wait. She never usually had any time to do something just for herself, so she decided she may as well make the most of it.

She put on her trainers, scraped her hair back into a pony tail and walked round to her parents' house.

"Hello love! Come in." Her mother was surprised to see her on a Saturday late afternoon. "Where are the kids?!"

"Oh Mum" Emma wrapped her arms round her mum's neck and nuzzled into her like she did when she was a child, only then she was much smaller than her mum and wrapped them round her hips then.

Over a cup of tea and a plate of biscuits, Emma explained to her mum what had happened, and although she didn't know exactly what was going on in Dan's head, she said that things hadn't been right for a wee while. Never in a million years did she ever expect him to do anything like this: upping and leaving with the kids was something she could never imagine him doing. They had always been a solid family unit. They done everything together. And now he won't even answer his phone to her.

"Do you want to go shopping and for lunch, love? On me? Maybe cheer you up a little bit?"

"No thanks, Mum. But I was thinking there is something you and dad can do to help, if you are free at all?"

Emma showed her mum the inspiration post she had seen earlier. It was an old post that one of the pages she followed had shared, where the girl had done up her living room on a tight budget "Back to when it all started" was the caption.

"I want to make my house a home. It just doesn't feel like me. I don't like it at all." She sobbed. "Don't get me wrong. I LOVE our house, and all of the memories it holds. But I just want something to be proud of."

"Of course, love" comforted her mum, ready to pass her a tissue in one hand, and her cuppa in the other – not sure which Emma would need more. "We don't have anything on today anyway, and it would be lovely to spend some time with you."

Emma's mum reached into her top kitchen drawer, pulled out her trusty pen and pad of paper and set about drawing out the shape of Emma's living room, detailing where the windows, door and radiator was positioned. A blank canvas. They played around with the lay out of the sofas, and by swapping them around they created a little more space. They talked budgets, colour schemes, and the overall vibe Emma craved.

They scrolled market place and found two matching sideboards free to the first person that came to collect them. Although they were dark brown wood and not the look she was going for, a little bit of time and TLC might just make them into something special. She picked up her phone and called the number. The man told her that he wasn't in at the moment, but he had left them outside and if they were still there then she could have them.

It was a risk but she had nothing to lose. She and her dad hopped into his old work van and drove the 20 minutes to the nearby village. She knew they would probably be gone, but they were free and she hoped that just this once luck would be on her side. She followed the sat nav on her phone, and pulled up to the address but there was no sideboards to be seen. With a big sigh, and a look towards her dad with a petted lip, he patted her on the back and slipped his van back into first gear. But, just as he did, he noticed the sideboards sitting behind a parked van. Emma couldn't believe that they were still there, or that her dad somehow managed to even spot them!

They were very heavy, but with some clever angled parking and her dad's dad skills, they managed to get both of the sideboards into the van with nothing but thankful smiles and sheer determination.

Emma and her dad drove back to her house to drop off the sideboards. She walked up to the front door to unlock it whilst her dad opened up the back of the van to put the sideboards in the garage. She noticed that the kitchen lights were on and she heard someone filling the kettle. Without even taking off her shoes she ran right through "Dan!!!!!"

"Oh no, hi love. It's only me," her mum called through, just as she approached the kitchen door. "I thought I may as well get here and get the kettle on for you arriving back."

The look on Emma's face must have said more than she ever could, and her mum was right over giving her another motherly cuddle.

"I keep doing that mum, I keep thinking they are back but it's not them" she sobbed.

"I know love, I know. Just give him time." She wiped away the tears. "Look, come and see this."

They went into the living room and there was a spread of newly purchased items. There was a big tin of Egyptian Cotton paint, a tin of white furniture paint and 3 large matching white frames. "If any of this is the wrong stuff love, we can go nip back and change it. I just wanted to surprise you, pet."

"Oh mum, thank you so much! And the frames are perfect! How did you know to get me them?"

"I saw them on one of the pictures you showed me, love. I just had to pick them up when I saw them in the shop, I thought you'd like them!"

"I really do, mum…" Emma's eyes glistened as her mum grabbed her and squeezed her in a big motherly hug.

"Come on, we've got plenty to get on with!"

Emma nodded and picked up the sanding paper and went out into the garage. Together they started sanding down the new sideboards whilst her dad set to work moving the furniture and started painting the walls. Emma was always amazed at how fast her dad could do it. He didn't need to use masking tape for the edges like she and Dan did, his hand was as steady as you'd expect from someone who painted rooms for their whole working life. Two coats later, and a wee top-up coat of wood silk to the woodwork, and the room was looking brand new.

The three of them together moved the sofas to their new position, and Emma and her dad carried in the sanded sideboards and placed them either side of the tv. It looked ok, but something just wasn't right.

"What about putting the TV on the wall, love?" said her mum.

"That would be too much of a faff, Mum."

Her dad shook his head. "Not at all, I can have that up there in no time."

"Thanks Dad, I love the look of it but I don't want all the wires hanging down."

"Emma, I am a professional! I can conceal them for you if you want it up?"

"Oh Emma, it will look just like your pictures you showed me!" gushed her mum.

"If you're sure, and it's not too much work for you, Dad. I really don't want to put you out."

"Not at all, love." With a smile, Emma and her mum got to work painting the sideboards with the furniture paint, while her dad set about measuring the wall and drilling holes. A quick trip to the DIY shop later, and the bracket was on and the TV was mounted. A wee coat of paint to the sideboards had totally transformed the look of them! They went from looking drab and old to expensive and modern, with little more than a tin of paint and a little hard work.

Whilst the paint dried, Emma and her mum spent time organising all of the kid's downstairs toys, using baskets to keep all the different types together. One thing Emma had was lots of baskets! Whenever she seen them cheap, she picked a few up, and now more than ever she was glad she did. One sideboard was to be used for the girls' stuff, and the other for Jasper's. All of the toys that usually lived scattered in the living room were now stored away for easy access. *The perfect compromise* thought Emma. *I wish the kids were here to see it.*

After a very long and tiring, yet productive day, the room was decorated, rearranged, new furniture bought and upcycled. Emma could not believe what was possible in just one day.

Emma's dad drove to their local favourite take away and placed an order for their tea. It was already after 9pm and they hadn't eaten since the cup of tea and biscuits earlier in the afternoon. They had certainly built up an appetite!

While he was away, Emma collected up the bits and pieces that she had indulgently bought over the last few months and placed them in her new living room. The vases, pampas grass and candles decorated the room, and the scent of her overly expensive designer wax melts filled the space. Emma's mum came through, she had found some black and white photos of Emma, Dan and the kids and put them into the frames. With a few Velcro picture strips, the frames were placed on the wall along the back of the sofa. Emma couldn't help but cry tears of mixed emotions. She was extremely proud of what they had achieved, but she so wished that Dan and the kids were here to see it all.

She picked up her phone and was upset to see that there was not one missed call or message. She had hoped that Dan would have returned her call by now. Although it was late, she called him again hoping that she'd at least catch Jasper before he went to bed. But it just went straight to his answer machine again. She went to hang up as she had done every other time, but instead this time she left a message "Dan, please call me" she paused. Waiting, as if he was going to pick up the phone like they did on old movies. But there was nothing but silence. She sighed and hung up.

Just then, her dad opened the door with a steaming hot bag of Chinese food. "Wow, it looks like a completely different house now! I'd forgotten all about it for a second there" he said with a cheeky grin. Emma loved how he always tried to make her smile.

After a well-earned, delicious meal. Emma thanked her parents for everything and kissed them goodbye as they left. Exhausted, she went straight upstairs to bed and, despite everything, slept right through the night.

Chapter 26

The next morning, Emma woke up with a new sense of clarity. She showered and took her time getting ready in the strangely quiet house. The fact that she was able to shower alone for the entire time without someone coming into the bathroom was unheard of. But being able to dry her hair and put on some make up in the morning was just too much for her. She wished that the girls were here, their laughter filling the room. Or Jasper popping in for a wee cuddle as he liked to sometimes do. She longed for the life she had only a couple of days before.

She dressed in her good jeans, a shirt and her mac raincoat. She'd had it since before she met Dan. It was an oldie, but a goodie. She matched it with a pair of trainers, a spritz of her favourite perfume and a dab of Vaseline on her lips. She looked casual-chic with her minimal effort, but she caught sight of herself in the mirror and knew that Dan would appreciate the effort she had went to. Not with just how she looked, but how the living room looked too.

Dan had the car with him, so Emma found the bus timetable on line and made her way down to the bus stop. The bus wasn't due for half an hour yet, but she wanted to get there early to make sure she didn't miss it.

Dan's parents lived over an hour away. She couldn't remember the last time she'd been on a bus without the kids, the only reason they ever went on the bus was because the kids loved it. It was like an exciting day out for the three of them, just to ride on a bus. It always amused Emma that they appreciated something so mundane as a bus ride. She smiled with the memories of Jasper when he was only 2 or 3 years old, sitting smiling at the front of the top of the bus, holding onto the handle bar that ran horizontally along the middle of the window, his bum barely touching the seat to be able to reach it.

She tried to keep her thoughts off of the conversation that was about to happen – she didn't want to ruin the little make up that she had on. Instead, she thought of all of the good things about her family. Her reasons to wake up in the morning. Her reason for living.

When she finally arrived at her in-law's house. The path leading to the front door all of a sudden seemed very far away. She had to steady herself on the gate as she got a little bit dizzy and the butterflies swarmed around in her tummy. A big deep breath, and she took her first step towards getting her family back. She walked up the three steps and rang the door-bell.

The door opened with a wave of red curls that glistened as soon as the sunlight touched them. "Mummy!!!!!" yelled Fern as the sunlight caught her red hair and it glistened gold. Luna was quick on her tail! "Daddy told us you weren't coming to Granny and Grandads!" Emma faked her best faux smile and scooped the girls up in one fell swoop. She squeezed them tight like she hadn't seen them for a year, never mind less than 2 days. It felt much, much longer than that.

"Hello, Emma! Good to see you" embraced Debbie with a cuddle. "How are you? Let me take your coat. Would you like a cup of tea?"

"I would adore one, thanks. I am parched!"

Debbie filled the kettle and set out 2 cups. "Does Dan know you're here?" she questioned cautiously, not knowing how to tread the situation.

"Erm, not exactly. I thought he'd return my call yesterday but he didn't. I was scared he'd tell me not to come."

"Ah, I see. Well, he and Tom are off to play football at the park with Jasper. The girls and I were just about to bake some shortie biscuits."

It was then that Emma noticed that the big food processor was out and all of the ingredients were on the worktops. She glanced down to look at her girls' who hadn't left her side and noticed that they had aprons on ready to start. "Oh, I am sorry, I didn't mean to interrupt. I just missed everyone so much, I just had to   see   you   all."

"Do not be sorry, I would have done exactly the same thing" Debbie poured the boiling water into the mugs and stirred them well. Steam, evaporating into the air in swirls, imitating the movement of the butterflies in her tummy had started to settle somewhat. "We'll have these cups of tea and then we can all bake together, how about that?!"

The girls squealed in delight, and Emma was so thankful for a mother-in-law like Debbie. Any mother could have taken their son's side; could have shut the door in her face out of loyalty to her son. Heaven knows that Emma probably would for Jasper, too. But Debbie was one of the kindest souls she had ever met, and she raised a son as good as Dan. Only a special kind of person can raise as good a father and a husband as he is. Was. *Eugh*. The thought of things potentially ending made Emma feel sick and she tried her best to put a brave smile on and bake the biscuits with her girls. *Think happy thoughts, think happy thoughts.*

The mantra worked. Emma had flour on her nose and the 4 of them were giggling away as though nothing was wrong when the front door opened.

"Mmm something smells good!" shouted through Dan as he kicked off his shoes and ran into the kitchen pretending to steal the shortie as it cooled, the girls whacking his hands away like they were playing Whac-a-mole. It took him a minute to realise that Emma was there, or, indeed, that she shouldn't be.

It was only when Jasper shouted "Mum!" and ran over to her that it clicked. "What are you doing here?" he smiled the biggest, half adult, half-child toothed smile at her. She roughed up his hair with her hand as she always did and gave him a big kiss on the cheek.

"Yes, Emma, what are you doing here?" Dan mirrored Jasper. Only, his question was much firmer than his son's.

This was not how this conversation was supposed to happen. Emma smiled "Can we speak outside?"

Dan walked out of the kitchen and Emma followed, quietly closing the door behind then. Dan walked out of the front door and onto the steps outside so that the family couldn't hear the conversation.

"Why are you here?" Dan asked again, this time with more assertiveness than he did in the kitchen when they had company.

"Dan, are you kidding me? I haven't heard from you, I called you umpteen times, I left a message for you with your mum, I left a message on your answering machine. And I have heard nothing back."

"I told you I needed time to think" he said bluntly.

"Dan, you just took the kids. You upped and left. You didn't even give me a chance to speak about anything." She sounded firmer than she felt. Her legs were like jelly.

"I know, I just needed to go. I had to think quickly, Emma. I wanted to give you the time and space to think about everything. And you know my mum and dad love spending time with the kids." At least he sounded like he still cared, just a little now. Rather than the defensive, almost aggressive way he was at the start of the conversation, thought Emma.

"You should have just spoken to me about all this, though, Dan. It doesn't make any sense. One minute, everything is fine, and the next minute you have all deserted me."

"Everything was fine?" he asked. "Emma, you have ignored me for weeks. You have changed completely. At first you were just off with me, but then when you started on the kids something had to be done. I couldn't bear the thought of you taking it out on them all October holidays. I just packed their stuff, picked them up early from school and came to my mums."

"Dan, I can't believe you would do that to me."

"I never thought I'd ever have to either, Emma."

"Just come home, Dan." She stepped forward to take his hand. He kept them firmly in his pocket. Rejected, she took a step backwards.

"I told you, Emma. I need time to think, too."

Her eyes welled up.

"We are going to stay here a little while longer. I really think you need to think about what you want, Emma. Because if it's not us, then it's not fair." Dan was talking with a sternness in his voice she had never heard before. "I am not having you taking out whatever it is that you are going through out on the kids."

"Dan, you know I would never do anything to harm them. Ever. They are my everything!"

"Emma, it's not the worst idea in the world. A few days thinking time. For us both. For us all."

Emma suddenly was aware of the snot that was now pouring from her nose, and the black smears from mascara tears that lined her finger tips. Goodness knows what her face must look like.

Dan gave her a hug. Not his usual, embracing hug. More of a friendly, comforting pat on the back type. Emma shrunk a little with it. She nodded her head and motioned towards the downstairs toilet as she wasn't sure what type of noise would come out if she opened her mouth to speak.

She locked the door behind her and splashed water on her face and glanced up at the mirror. The mascara was running down her cheeks and water alone was not enough to remove it. She got a scrunch of toilet roll and scrubbed away at the mascara marks as it disintegrated in her hands. She opened the window to let the fresh air cool her down and she tried to inhale as much of it as she could to calm herself down. This was not how this was supposed to go. With a final deep breath, she readied herself to exit the bathroom.

Emma said her goodbyes to the kids as briefly as she could. It was the hardest thing she ever had to do and it took every ounce of her being not to cry in front of them.

"Granny and Grandad are so happy you are staying and would like you to stay for a few more days! I have got a lot of things to do at home, but I will see you all soon. I will be at home waiting for you. You can videocall me any time you want to see me."

And with a kiss and a cuddle to each of her three beautiful babies, Emma left her in-laws house not sure if she would ever kiss or cuddle her husband ever again. Her heart broke in two.

Chapter 27

Nicola

Slowly but surely, Nicola was starting to feel better. Not just back to normal, but actually better; a better version of herself. She was still nowhere near where she wanted to be, but she was well on the road to it. She had more time to herself, more time for others, she was healthier and she was happier. Happier than she'd been in a long time.

From the outside, it didn't look like that though. She was still officially off sick from her work from having a break-down. But she could feel it and the excitement for the possibilities that lay ahead of her.

She spent the whole day out walking. She wasn't walking anywhere in particular; she just went wherever her feet wanted to take her. She had recently discovered that she really enjoyed people watching. She was fascinated in the way people moved around her, and how they interacted with the people around them. She watched an old man feeding the ducks in sheer delight. She saw families at the park, with mothers adoring their children. She revelled in couples walking, holding hands whilst out walking their dog. She imagined where they had been, where they were going, what they were talking about or thinking. She tried to guess where they lived, and what their jobs were. And although she was probably a million miles from the truth, she took great pleasure in her little guessing game.

That evening, she followed her feet as they took her up the hill. On her descent down she saw a woman slightly younger than herself sitting on a big rock admiring the view and deep in thought. She was drawn to her, she wondered what she was looking at, what she was thinking. The woman was there for a while and she geared herself up to strike up conversation. She didn't know why she was compelled to do so and it was so out of character for her. *What a nice night for a walk? No. Everything looks so small, doesn't it? No, not that either.*

Just as she was thinking what to say, she sat down next to her and the woman placed her hand on top of hers. She looked straight into her face in sheer horror. Straight away Nicola recognised her, she was one of the dinner ladies at school and although she had never had a direct conversation with her, she knew exactly who she was. But by the look on her face, she didn't know who Nicola was.

"Hi, Emma!?"

"What? WHAT?! Who are you?!" she was panicking.

"Emma, it's me. Calm down. It's Nicola."

"Nicola? I don't know a Nicola!" Emma frantically started shouting.

Nicola took a step closer so that Emma could see who it was.

Emma looked backwards and forwards and started stomping down the hill, leaving her belongings behind.

Jeez, she must really be in a hurry!

"Emma, you forgot this!" Nicola started following quickly behind with her flask. "I'll walk you down. It's a beautiful night for a walk, and some company."

The shared the walk down the hill together and as much as Nicola enjoyed people watching and wondering what they were up to, tonight she really enjoyed the company. *It would be good to get to know her a little more,* thought Nicola. Then she realised that she hadn't had a reply from her about the BBQ. She really hoped she included her in the message.

"Did you get my message about Saturday? I hope you can make it!"

"Oh yes, sorry, I have a kid's party. Sorry I can't!"

"That's such a shame, I was really hoping you could make it!" Nicola couldn't hide the disappointment in her voice. "OK, well, maybe next time! This is me here, I will see you next week, if not before!"

"See you then. Bye!"

Nicola watched as Emma walked in the opposite direction to where she was headed.

Chapter 28

Emma

Emma had no money to spend so couldn't go out with her friends. Not that they would be free anyway, they would be on days out with their own families. And after spending the whole day before with her parents, she didn't want to bother them anymore than she already had. So, with another day to herself, Emma decided to give the house a deep clean.

She started in her own bedroom. She had clothes that she hadn't even looked at for years and had long forgotten about. She emptied her wardrobe and chest of drawers and made 3 piles: keep, bin and charity shop. Her categories were very black and white, and Emma was in a ruthless mood. She only kept things that she loved, and that fitted her well. If it didn't look good on or she didn't feel amazing in it, then it was relegated from the keep pile. If it was in good condition, it went into the charity shop pile, and if it had seen better days, then it ended up in the bin pile.

A couple of hours later, all of the clothes in Emma's room had been sorted out and either put back into her wardrobe or put into bin bags, of which there were six: 4 for charity shops, and 2 for the bin. She didn't even know she owned that many clothes. And God knows she'd never get the chance to wear them all anyway. Now, her wardrobe was full of clothes that she loved, and plenty space to see what it was that she actually had. Her chest of drawers could now open and close easily, without having to push down the mountain of clothes while simultaneously pushing it just to be able to get it shut. She felt a huge satisfaction at the task she had completed. She opened her bedroom window and lay on her bed letting the cool autumn breeze blow over her. And as it did, she wanted to capture this fresh feeling, and let her bedroom imitate it.

She went downstairs and opened the tin of Egyptian Cotton paint. There was about a quarter left. Not enough to do the whole room, but definitely enough for a feature wall. She pulled back the bed, put masking tape over the edges of the wall to protect the other walls and woodwork. She painted a thin coat onto the wall and instantly the room looked better already.

Whilst the paint dried, she sorted out Jaspers room. It was far from being bad. Everything he had was in order. His whole room was neat and tidy, unless he was in the middle of a building spree. But he did have toys in drawers that he hadn't looked at since he started school. She got an old plastic storage box and filled it with all of his old toy cars, wooden building blocks, and Duplo sets. She smiled and cried happy tears as she filled the box with the memories of her beautiful little boy. She hadn't realised how quickly he had grown up. Before the girls came along, she spent all of her time with her little bestie and his chubby little face. It was like he had grown up all of a sudden to a tween.

She closed her eyes at the thought of him growing up before her very own eyes. She dusted his shelves and surfaces and smoothed out his bedsheets. His bedroom looked perfect. Well, as perfect as it could, without him in it, of course. She wiped her tears on her sleeve, remembering that she would one day in the very near future, be feeling the same way about the age he is now. He is only 8 years old, after all. She vowed to treasure every moment with him, and still remember that he really is still very little.

The next room to tackle was Fern and Luna's room. It was a stark contrast from their big brother's. Their room was cluttered with toys, clothes and trinkets. The girls loved to play, they loved pink and they loved clothes. This room took a lot longer than Jaspers and her own, and that included doing the painting!

After a few hours, Emma's tummy rumbled. It was becoming a habit of going all day on cup of tea and a biscuit, it seemed. She went down to the fridge and was ever so thankful for the leftover Chinese takeaway that her mum had kept for her.

She took out the dishes, opened the corner of the plastic lids and put them in the microwave until they were piping hot. Suddenly ravenous, she scooped up a spoonful of chicken curry and burned her tastebuds doing so. She had to blow on her plate, just like she used to for all three of her kids. And with that thought, more tears streamed down her face. She thought she would have been all cried out by now but it appeared not. How could Dan not know what it was that Emma wanted. It was all she wanted. Her family to be together. They were happiest when they were together. They told each other that all the time. And it was true. The Millars loved spending time together. Even the boring stuff was fun when they were together. What was it exactly that Dan needed time to think about?

As soon as the food had cooled down enough, Emma took a few more spoonful's and found that she was full. Her appetite had diminished as quickly as it had appeared. She popped her head in the girls' bedroom door to admire her work. The LOL doll house and the Barbie doll houses were set up expertly, just how the girls liked them. All of their old, broken and unloved toys were placed into two plastic storage tubs, one for the bin and one for the charity shop. The room looked amazing. She had never noticed how cute it looked before. Although it was still "busy," the rainbow wallpaper done an excellent job of tying in all of the colours of the toys in the room. The girls were lucky to have all that they did. Emma was lucky to have them. She closed the door and the thoughts began to race through her mind again and she tried to convince herself that the girls were enjoying themselves and having some quality time with their grandparents, that was all. They would be back soon.

She went back into her own bedroom and lightly touched the freshly painted wall. It was dry to the touch, so she set up and gave it another quick coat. Pleased with how it looked, and how quickly she managed to do it, she pulled off the masking tape. The satisfaction of pulling it off put a little smile on her face. She pushed back her bed a bit, but not too close to the wall. It was a few hours until bedtime yet. But it had been a long day. Emma was physically and emotionally drained. Going to bed now though, would mean that she'd be up again in the middle of the night and that was the last thing Emma wanted. She wanted to keep her mind off of what was going on and keep busy. She didn't need time to think, she scowled as she thought back to her earlier conversation with Dan.

Emma pulled on her trainers, and covered in speckles of greige paint, she went for a walk in the cool evening October air. Emma wasn't really one for noticing the weather or being overly concerned with it. Whether it was warm, or cold, she would dress herself and the kids appropriately. It didn't particularly make a difference to her if it was summer, or autumn. It was just a day with weather like the rest of them. But tonight, Emma noticed the crunch of leaves underfoot. She took a deep breath in and felt her lungs fill with the fresh, welcome chill in the air. The summer had been so hot and muggy, but this feeling of fresh, coolness seemed to wrap itself around her in a calming embrace.

Before long, Emma found herself in town. And to her surprise, a little shop was glowing in the dusky evening. As she drew closer, she seen it was a little coffee shop she hadn't spotted before. She put her hand into her pocket and pulled out the change from her earlier unsuccessful bus journey. The journey itself, was a success per se. But the destination, and indeed outcome, was not. Although she didn't have the money to spare, she decided that she deserved a little treat after the day she'd had. She walked in and looked up at the massive chalk-board menu, and then down at the change in her hand. It was only £2.70. It wasn't enough for anything on the menu.

"Can I help you?" asked the barista.

Embarrassed, Emma glanced up from her change "Erm, no thank you, I was just looking" and popped her money back into her pocket and went to turn on her heels and walk straight back out.

"This one is free" called the young girl. "The customer before you wanted to pay it forward. It's already been paid for. Please, what would you like?"

Emma smiled and blinked away the tears that were starting to form. "Erm, I will take your seasonal special, please."

"Excellent, is that to sit in or take away?" the barista smiled a caring smile.

"To take away please."

The steaming hot pumpkin spice latte was poured into the cup and the lid popped on, and Emma recognised the "I like you a Latte" cup from Instagram. She picked up the cup and went to put her change into the tips jar. "I am sorry, I don't have enough to do a pay it forward, but please take what I do have."

"No, no, it's ok, you keep it." said the barista. She realised that if Emma didn't have enough money for a cup of coffee, then she probably needed it more than she did.

"You and the pay it forward stranger have showed me so much kindness just when I needed it, and for that I am really grateful" and Emma popped the money into the jar.

The coffee warmed Emma up from the inside, and she appreciated every sip of the delicious, creamy, frothy spiced drink on her cool, brisk walk. By the time she got home, she felt so much better. She lit a few candles in the living room and popped on a film. And for the first time in a long time, she didn't scroll the internet whilst she did. She enjoyed the moment for what it was, as much as she could considering the circumstances.

That night, both Emma and the barista went to bed with their hearts a little happier than they would have done if it weren't for their coffee shop encounter.

Chapter 29

By the end of the week, Emma had had several video calls with the kids. They seemed to be having a great time, but there was no sign of them coming home yet. It's not that she hadn't spoken to Dan, but the conversations were always very short, and always in front of the kids. So, she didn't get the chance to speak to him properly. The one time she did ask if they could speak in private, he asked her to respect his wishes for some thinking time. It hurt her so much to feel him slipping from her fingers the way he was, as though it was in slow motion but there wasn't anything she could seem to do to stop him.

The kids had been enjoying themselves with their grandparents. They had been fishing and Jasper couldn't stop talking about it, how many fish he caught and how he had learned how to set it all up and reel them in. He was saying, though, that the girls squealed and ran away whenever a fish was caught. They preferred sitting at the bench drinking cups of hot chocolate and playing with their Barbies while their granny completed her crossword puzzle.

They had been swimming at the local public pool since their lessons were off for the holidays. Granny and Grandad had also taken them shopping and kitted them out with new clothes and winter coats. They baked, they played, they drew. They were just having a great time and Emma couldn't deny it. She wanted to be with her family too but Dan was insistent on the space and thinking time.

Every time Emma thought about it, she would produce a new theory as to what he was thinking about. It went from he didn't love her any more – but that didn't make sense because just a few weeks before he was buying her flowers and cuddling into her at bedtime and actually just not leaving her alone. Almost suffocating her, at times. So it couldn't be that.

Then she thought that he must have someone else. If he wasn't getting anything from her then he must of went somewhere else to satisfy his needs. But then she thought that if that was what he was up to, then he certainly wouldn't have gone to his parents' house and taken the kids with him.

But her final, and current, theory was that he was going to divorce her. He was giving himself time away from her to see if he could manage to deal with the kids without her; to give him space to realise if that were what he actually wanted before he made it official. Whenever Emma thought about it, she got shooting pains up her knuckles and she felt nauseous at the thought. So whenever that thought began to bubble up, she pushed it aside and thought of something else. And whenever that didn't work, she put in her headphones, put on her trainers and went out for a long walk.

She found herself going for walks more often. Now that it was a week into the October Holidays and the house was deep cleaned, decluttered and looking better than it ever had, she didn't have much else to do.

She had spent the previous days sorting out the kitchen and bathroom. She had chucked out old spices and tins of food that were years out of date. She cleaned out the fridge and defrosted the freezer. She spent a whole day batch-cooking healthy meals and filled the freezer with enough meals to feed a small army on a very tight budget. She cleared out every cupboard, wiped it all down and only kept what she actually used. With more space in the drawers and cupboards, she was able to put away lots of items that sat out on the worktops. It made such a difference, the kitchen actually looked bigger and much cleaner. Emma realised that it actually wasn't as bad as she once thought it was. It was a modern, plain kitchen with good worktops. It was just too cluttered to see before. With clear worktops and a candle lit, she actually quite liked it.

The bathroom was quite dated. Not in an avocado 3-piece suite type of way, but more of a less-than-metro-tiles-and-sleek-black-accessories kind of way. It was a plain, white bathroom, with white floor tiles and white walls. The shelves were filled with toiletry bottles, miniatures from holidays past and the odd hotel stay. Rather than examining each item, Emma decided to just put aside everything that was frequently used and binned the rest. Goodness knows how long it had all been there anyway, but one thing is for sure, the dust that lay on the lids and shoulders of some of the bottles demonstrated that it was way too long.

With her family gone, she had nothing. Every day she had kept herself busy sorting the house out, but now that was done. Emma felt lost. After a long walk in the morning, Emma spent the afternoon on the sofa watching another film. She couldn't watch a rom-com though, she had tried earlier in the week and it had made her feel awful. Her whole body ached for what she didn't have. Instead, she found herself watching murder documentaries and horror films. Not her usual cup of tea, and not something she ever thought she'd be in to, especially now that she was staying in the house on her own. But some part of her felt better watching them but she didn't know why. Maybe it was because it made her realise that things could be much worse. Or maybe it was just the simple fact that it made her forget about her own troubles and worry about someone else's. Either way, it made the time pass quicker. That afternoon, Emma found herself nestling down for the afternoon with a series of Unsolved Murder Mysteries and a hot cup of tea.

Having had no actual company for almost a week now, Emma decided to call her mum. They had tried to call each other a few times over the past few days but kept missing each other. But tonight, Emma wondered if they would be free for her to pop round for tea.

"Hi love, how are you? What did Dan and the kids think of their new living room?" asked her mum, slightly out of breath.

"Where are you, Mum?"

"Oh remember, me and your dad are away for our anniversary. We're booked in for a few nights away near Edinburgh. We're just walking along the beach to get some fish and chips now."

"Oh, so you are, Mum. I totally forgot...I will let you go and enjoy your walk! I'll catch you later. Love you." Emma hung up the phone as quickly as she could. She wasn't ready to talk about her situation yet, and she didn't want her parents to be worrying about her on their wee break away. She thought it would have been long resolved by now, and she'd be spending her holiday with her family just like she had planned to. Instead, she was spending it all alone and on the verge of a divorce.

Oh well, a tin of tomato soup and another walk it is then, thought Emma. She heated up her soup and poured it into a flask. This late afternoon she decided on a different route. She walked out of the city streets and into the forest. She started walking up the hill, through the trees and up a dried muddy path speckled with stones and fallen leaves. It was a beautiful walk, Emma felt as though she was in the middle of the country side. She made a promise to herself to do this more often.

Clambering up and getting slightly out of breath, she found a vista between the trees and sat herself down on a rock to admire the view. The city seemed far below her, further than the 20 minute walk that it took to get there. She could see her house, the school and her local shops. At the other side of the city, she could see the big fancy houses that she always dreamed of having.

As the sun set it lit up the whole city with a warm, orange glow. Emma realised that it didn't actually matter what side of town you lived in. The sun still shone on each house equally. Each house had just as much a chance of being a happy family home as the other. And similarly, each house also had the same amount of chance to be lonely. It didn't matter how many bricks your house was made of. All that mattered was what was inside them. Emma opened her flask and sipped on the warm, tomato soup. It warmed her from the inside out and she appreciated the simplicity for all that it was. She closed her eyes and felt the sun warm her face and slowly cool as it disappeared below the horizon. She opened her eyes and was shocked at how dark it had gotten so quickly. The stars scattered across the sky like diamonds on an almost black velvet blanket, she couldn't believe just how beautiful and sparkly they were from up here. She decided she better head back home before it got really dark and put her hand on the rock to push herself up and begin her descent back down the hill. But instead of touching the rock, she put her hand on top of someone else's hand and let out a blood- curdling scream.

"Aaaaaaahhhhhh! What the hell!!!!!!?" as she realised someone had been sitting next to her on the rock.

"Hi Emma!?" a cool, calm voice replied.

"What? WHAT?! Who are you?!" Emma's heart was beating out of her chest so loudly she was sure the stranger could hear it. An afternoon of watching murder documentaries had certainly taken its toll on her.

"Emma, it's me. Calm down. It's Nicola."

"Nicola? I don't know a Nicola!" Emma frantically started shouting.

Nicola took a step closer so that Emma could see who it was.

The blood drained from her face as she realised that it was the head teacher Nicola Smythe. The one person who made her feel awful just to even be in her presence, had seen her at her most vulnerable state. *Things just really couldn't get any worse.* Emma started to pace backwards and forwards, unsure of what to do. If she should speak to her, if she should just walk away back down the hill and head home. Yes, that's what she wanted to do, and she started walking away without saying another word.

"Emma, you forgot this!" Nicola started following quickly behind with her flask. "I'll walk you down. It's a beautiful night for a walk, and some company."

Nicola smiled at Emma for what must have been the first time, and she didn't know how to take it. The conversation they had as they walked down the hill together was actually enjoyable. Just before they parted ways, Nicola stung her with the question she had been dreading all along.

"Did you get my message about Saturday? I hope you can make it!"

Emma quickly made an excuse about having a kid's party.

"That's such a shame, I was really hoping you could make it!" It didn't seem patronising. *But could she really be genuine?*

Chapter 30

Emma

Saturday morning came with a burst of sunlight under the blinds and Emma woke up with a good feeling about the day. Without even realising it, she was smiling before she opened her eyes. She rolled over, jumped out of bed and smoothed her bed sheets and pulled up her duvet to make her bed perfectly: each cushion placed just-so. She smoothed her hands over the cover and felt its softness skim her hands. It was crease free and looked so comfortable and inviting. *Dan will appreciate this when he gets home,* and with that thought, she thoroughly brushed her teeth and went straight downstairs, half expecting to see Dan and the kids sitting at the table with their special Saturday morning breakfast spread.

As she got closer to the kitchen, she realised that she could not hear the excited chatter of her kids. *Or maybe they are just hiding to surprise me,* she thought. But she opened the door, and to her disappointment they weren't there yet. So, on her way upstairs to get ready, she went into each room to check that everything was still in its place. It looked great, she had to admit. So tidy and fresh looking. A clear out really made all of the difference. Now she just needed to fill the place with her chaos again. Her perfectly, imperfect chaos.

She peeled off her pyjamas and dropped them into the empty washing basket. Although she missed her husband and her children dearly, she had to admit that it was nice that the house was always spotless and everything was left exactly as she left it. She had no one to clean up after. The laundry was more than manageable. So manageable, in fact that the basket never filled up. Everything was where it belonged and all that the house needed was a wee dust, clean and hoover every so often. Still, it had been over a week now since they had left. Dan had said it would only be a few days. Today had to be the day that they'd all be home.

She ran herself a hot shower, washed her hair and made sure she was silky smooth all over. She enjoyed her final shower completely in peace, she even put the radio on as she did to fully savour the experience.

She dried her hair and clipped it back in a clasp. She wore her comfy leggings and a big baggy woollen jumper. Although she looked very comfy and casual, the little make up that she put on elevated her look. A base of tinted moisturiser, a smudge of blush and a lick of mascara, Emma looked and felt good and was ready for her heart to be healed. She had butterflies for the second time this week. Although instead of nerves and anxiety, this time it was with excitement.

She picked up her phone to call Dan expecting him to answer, but he rejected her call. Strange, she tried again. Rejected again. Maybe it is because this wasn't a rearranged call, like the video calls to the kids were. She called Debbie's number instead. Apparently, Dan was out for the day with the kids.

"He isn't ready to see you just yet, Emma. I know I probably shouldn't be saying anything. The last thing I want to do is get between you and Dan, but I really don't want to pick sides either" muttered Debbie as she talked quietly down the phone.

"Ok, Debbie. I understand. Thank you. Can you please just tell him I called." Emma's eyes nipped as she hung up the phone. She couldn't believe that they weren't coming home today. Although she had begun to enjoy some slithers of her alone time, she was ready for it all to be over and things to return to normal. She sobbed big fat tears as she berated herself for even allowing hope to build up that things would be ok again. Now the doubts of divorce that she worked hard to keep at bay started to flood in.

She shoved on her trainers, locked the door behind her and started running. She didn't know where she was going, or why she was even running – she hadn't ran since she was at school. But she just had to get away from it all. Away from the house. Away from the feelings. Away from herself.

The tears of hurt and disappointment turned to rage. Every step on the pavement was a release of anger. She thudded as she ran through the streets, passed the fields and into the forest. Before long Emma found herself at the vista again, over-looking the city. The tears had dried up and now she was just pissed off. She sat on the rock and went over everything in her head.

He had hurt her, deserted her, and embarrassed her. She had tried to speak to him but he was having none of it. *How dare he.* Tomorrow, Emma decided she was going to get her kids back. If he didn't want her, then fine. But there was no way on this entire Earth that she was going to let him keep her kids. *Over my dead body.*

Emma decided that as they were on a day out today, she would let him have it. His final little perfect bubble he so clearly wanted. But tomorrow, she was taking back what was hers. But today, she needed a good bloody drink.

In that very moment, she was brought right back to her conversation with Nicola at that very same spot. Her mind was made up.

Emma ran right back down the hill and went via the supermarket on her way home. She picked up a bottle of pink gin and a 2 litre bottle lemonade. *May as well go out with a bang,* thought Emma. Kill two birds with one stone. She decided that no-one was going to make her feel worthless ever again. She would go to the BBQ and tell Nicola exactly what she thought of her. She didn't owe her anything. She went to work to do a job, get paid and come home. That was it. Never again would she let anyone have that power over her.

Then in the morning, she would get her kids back, no matter what.

And her life would be sorted.

Chapter 31

Nicola

Nicola, Donna and Jackie met at "I Like You a Latte" as planned on Friday at 10am. They all brought their laptops, notepads, and were dressed in comfy-casual clothes. They meant business! They ordered coffee after coffee and were served a round of cakes and pastries on the house, probably due to the amount of money they were spending on coffee alone. Or perhaps, it's because they had to be eaten that day or they'd be thrown out. No one knew. But either way, Nicola appreciated the generosity.

The main areas that Nicola had proposed were Resources, Working Time Agreement (WTA) and Staff Wellbeing. They divided up the main areas, and each woman lead their own area with Jackie on Resources, Donna on the WTA and Nicola on overall Staff Wellbeing.

Jackie spent her time creating a bank of resources for each of the areas of the curriculum. Teachers spend so much of their own time planning and preparing resources. One would assume that the resources would be available for teachers to just pick up and go, but that is not the case. The teacher creates the lesson, trying to make it as fun and as engaging as possible, whilst ensuring that the individual needs of each child are being met. This means differentiating the resources accordingly. And the teacher doesn't just have to do this once per day. They have to do it for every single lesson, for every single day. With around 6 lessons per day, and 5 days a week. That is over 30 lessons to plan, prepare and differentiate for. By having a bank of resources available, this would alleviate the need for teachers to spend their own time searching for and creating lessons and resources. Sure, it would cost the school money to have this available to all. But, in the long run, it would save them so much more.

This links directly to Donna's area of expertise – the WTA. With only 7 hours per week allocated to teachers planning and preparation time, that actually only gives 14 minutes per lesson. If only! No wonder teachers feel overwhelmed and underpaid! Nicola shared her analogy of her salary being split into an hourly rate; she'd be better off stacking shelves at the supermarket. The three of them laughed at the irony of it all. Donna amended the WTA to fairly reflect the teachers' workload. She had taken out anything that could be deemed as unnecessary and gave the required time to plan and prepare for lessons.

Nicola worked tirelessly on the general staff wellbeing area of her improvement plan. She wanted to inspire and invigorate her staff as well as being able to provide them with the tools to be able to support themselves, and cope when necessary. She found some of the best training modules and speakers available and booked them throughout the rest of the school year and made sure that the training and events were all accounted for within the new WTA.

Nicola loved that the three of them were sitting here, all working hard in their own time. Not because they wanted to, or because they had nothing else better to do, but because they cared. They cared about their staff, and they cared about all of the pupils.

After a few hours in the coffee shop, the women became a team. They were a strong team before, but now they were all aligned with the same goal and heading in the same direction. Nicola finally felt ready to return back to school with a bang.

Chapter 32

It was the morning of the BBQ. It was wet, cold and windy. NOT the type of weather you want for a party in the garden. Nicola checked the weather for the 100th time, the rain was due to be off by lunch, and without wanting to jinx it, it was supposed to be quite warm. Nicola prayed that the weather forecast was true, but right now, it didn't look so great.

Regardless, the party was going ahead. The food delivery arrived and Nicola had booked in the cleaner for an extra clean on Friday – just to make sure that everything was spic n span. *I really do need to remember to thank James for that one – having a cleaner really did make life so much easier,* she thought.

So now that everything was done, she spent the morning getting ready. She put music on, danced in the shower, and enjoyed trying on her clothes in a little fashion show just like she used to many moons ago prior to a night out. *How life was different since then,* she thought.

Just when she'd decided on an outfit, she seen the parcel neighbour across the road come out of her house. She pulled on her leggings and jumper and ran out, hoping to catch her before she went out. She just made it.

"Hi, I was hoping I would catch you today!"

There was no response. Nicola wasn't expecting this, after her smile the other week, she thought she'd be forthcoming. Still, she supposed she couldn't expect any more really considering the experiences they have had together.

"I have chapped on your door a few times but no one was ever in."

Parcel woman nodded yet there was still no response.

"I am having a barbecue this afternoon and I would really appreciate it if you could come? I feel we got off on the wrong foot, and I would love to make it up to you?"

"Oh, I am sorry, but I already have plans, I am about to go down to my mums."

"Bring her too if you like?! It's just my family, a few work colleagues and some neighbours coming. Nothing too big. But I would really love it if you could come? It starts at 2pm. It would be lovely to see you."

"Thanks so much for the invite. I will see what I can do."

Nicola was hopeful. She really wanted to make it up to her and get to know her. They were neighbours, after all.

Just then, Nicola saw her sons coming back home from playing football with their friends.

"Ah there they are, my two favourite boys in the whole wide world!"

"Stop it mum, someone will hear you" Jamie joked back.

"Right you two, showers, now. Everyone will be here soon, and you two are filthy!"

Nicholas wrapped his arm round his mum's shoulder. Jamie followed suit. And it was then, for the first time she noticed how tall the boys actually were. Nicholas was almost as tall as she was, and Jamie wasn't far behind him.

"Soon enough, and you boys will be towering over me!"

"And then it will be us two in charge!"

"Yeah, right! You could be as tall at the Eiffel Tower and I would still be the boss! Now, shower, and get dressed. Your clothes are laying on your beds!"

As big as they were, they were still only children, and Nicola intended to treat them as children for as long as she could. Time really was ticking before they'd refuse to wear the clothes, she picked out for them, or before she could tell them when to shower or when to come home."

The rainclouds had parted, the sun was shining in its bright blue sky. James and the boys set up the garden as Nicola directed where she wanted everything to go. She had planned several different seating areas to accommodate all of the guests and she had even "borrowed" some chairs from the school to make sure that there was enough seats for everyone.

The boys were in charge of the playlist, but Nicola had a few "golden oldies" as they liked to call them, that must be included. The rest of the songs were up to them. The boys linked the speakers up through Bluetooth and were ready to go.

The food was laid out in a massive spread across the island in the kitchen. She had the oven on to pre-cook the chicken, burgers and sausages ready to be finished on the BBQ later when the guests arrived. The make-shift bar was stocked up, buckets of ice and plastic glasses were perched on the table ready for everyone to help themselves. She looked at her family helping her, proud of all that they had achieved, not just now, but in the last couple of months. She couldn't have wished for a better family. No matter what she had put them through, they were still here for her, showing up. No matter what.

Just as she was about to get emotional, the back door gate opened.

"Helloooooo! We came a little bit early to see if you needed a hand" exclaimed Jackie.

"Aaaaand to give you one of these – we thought you might be needing one!" Donna handed her a tin of pre-mixed cocktail, and she noticed that the girls were already drinking one each.

"Thank you so much, girls! You're right, I do need one, thanks! But I think we are all set and ready to go! Actually, there is one thing you can do for me, if you don't mind? James! Nicholas and Jamie! Come here!"

The three men in her life all came over, wondering what was going on.

"Can you take a picture of us, please. I don't know when the last time was that we had one all together."

"Oh mum" the boys chimed in chorus.

"Come on, for me."

The 4 of them stood together, Nicola and James were as proud as punch.

Nicola was glad she got the picture when she did because, from that moment on, more and more people filled the garden. Nicola spent the whole afternoon with each and every person that attended, conversing with them, telling jokes and offering them drinks and shots. She was surprised when Emma came through the gate with Julie. She caught her eye as she came in but was busy in conversation that she had to wait to get to her. By the time she got to her, she was surprised to see that Julie was gone, and she was sitting with Kali. She really wanted to impress the both of them, so she brought over the tray of shots and struck up conversation. She was truly grateful for their company, and them being here for her meant the world.

To Nicola, the party wasn't only a reward for her SLT for working during the holidays to get her new initiative up and running. It was so much more than that: it was a celebration of herself, of everyone she had and wanted in her life. It represented who she was, what she had been through, and the coming out of the other side. She had a new found respect for people; a better understanding of what people go through without anyone else ever knowing, like she did with her own mental health. She sincerely understood the delicate balance it took in running a life well. Sometimes it just took one minor thing to happen and everything could come crashing down around you. If it weren't for the love and support of her family, friends and colleagues, she wouldn't be the person she was today.

So every second, spent with every guest, Nicola wanted them to feel as special and as wanted as they were to her. She would never not appreciate anyone ever again.

When she was sure she had been around everyone, bringing fun and drinks and stories and chats with her. She paused the music through her phone.

"Hello. Hi. Hi! I just wanted to say thank you to everyone for coming today. As most of you will know, I haven't had the easiest time of it recently. My world came crashing down around me and I physically, emotionally or mentally could not continue life the way I had been." Although everyone was drinking and having fun, they all stopped and had their eyes on her. She glanced around everyone as she spoke, looking them in the eye in turn.

"I was cranky, emotional, and snappy to those that I love the most. And that was before the breakdown." There was a few stifled well-intended giggles.

"There were days I literally could not get out of bed. Days turned to night, and night turned to day and I didn't know where I was or what I was doing."

"When someone is deemed as successful, people think they are invincible to mental health issues. The truth is that no one is. Mental health problems do not discriminate. They really can happen to anyone. But I am one of the lucky ones. I got the support I needed. I managed to take time out and build better habits. I have seen the error in my ways, and I have vowed to myself that I won't ever be that person again."

"To my family, I would not be here if it weren't for you. James, you stood by me when others would have long walked away. You knew that my heart was in the right place, and that everything I done was for you, even if things weren't done the way you would have wanted them to be done, you went along with it anyway. And to my boys. You done the hardest things imaginable. You stood up to me. You taught me that just because I thought something was right, didn't mean that I got to call the shots for everyone. We are in this together. You three really are more important to me than anything else in the world and I promise I will do anything for you. It really isn't about being successful or having a big fancy house or flashy cars, at the end of the day none of that matters when you don't have your health and those that you love. I know we joke about it now, but I am your mum, not your boss." She blew her family a kiss and blinked back the tears.

"And on that note. To my wonderful staff, colleagues and friends. I promise to make our school not only the most sought after school for children, but also for the staff too. Your hard work and dedication to your profession and to the children does not go unnoticed. But the truth is, we all work way more than we are paid to do. Donna, Jackie and I have really tried to streamline things so that your job is as easy as possible."

Jackie and Donna raised their glasses and nodded their head towards Nicola.

"We want to make sure that all of the tools and resources you require for your job are already there, waiting for you to just pick up and go. There will be no unnecessary training or paperwork required, that the only meetings and trainings you are required to go to are actually beneficial to your role and the children. And that, without exception, you work no more than your contracted working hours. We will do everything in our power to make our school the place to be!"

"Amen to that!" shouted a chorus of teachers as they downed another shot.

"So everyone, one final thing I need to say; the most important thing is to look after yourself. Be kind to yourself and to those around you. Take time to do the things you enjoy, spend time with those you love. Really get to know yourself and prioritise that. As the saying goes, you cannot pour from an empty cup, and I have never really fully understood the meaning of that phrase until the last couple of months. Anyway, on that note. Being good to yourself also means taking the time and letting your hair down. So everyone, pour yourself another drink, have another bite to eat, sing, dance, and enjoy each other's company. I love you all."

The music started up again, not that you could hear it over everyone's cheers.

The party continued on from the afternoon and the boys crashed out around 11pm and went up to bed. They had never seen their mum let her hair down like this before. As much as they tried to, they just couldn't keep up with her.

The drink flowed, the food was eaten and the music was danced to. Nicola spent the rest of the night chatting and dancing with James and those that were left right through to the early hours of the morning.

She thinks she might have made two new special friends that night. At least, she hoped she did.

Chapter 33

Emma

Emma walked to the BBQ from her house. She had text a couple of the girls from her work to see if anyone was going. Of course Julie would be there, but she was only going at 2pm just to "show face" as she already had other plans, so Emma arranged to meet her there. None of the other girls were able to make it. When she walked in to the garden, Emma was thankful for the friendly face in a sea of unfamiliar faces. She sat down at a table with Julie and she poured herself a large gin while her friend sipped on a can of juice. Before she even finished her first drink, Julie answered her phone. Her lift was outside already so she had to go.

"Sorry, I wasn't even here half an hour! I'll catch up with you again with the kids over the holidays?"

"Definitely!" Emma promised, to herself, if not to Julie.

The two girls cuddled good bye and as Julie went away to her other social event, Emma downed her drink and poured herself another large gin.

The rest of the party seemed to be having fun, but Emma sat on her own. She hadn't even seen Nicola yet. She didn't care though; she would get what was coming to her. For now, Emma just wanted to forget.

"May I join you?" Emma looked up to see a beautiful young woman she thought she recognised, but not sure where from. She had a bottle of wine and offered her a glass.

"Yes, of course." She moved her coat out of the way to make room for the familiar face. She went to open the wine and realised she needed a corkscrew. She shortly returned with one and Emma realised what the wine was.

"Whispering Angel?!...I have wanted to try this for ages, are you sure you don't mind?" she blushed as she asked.

"Of course not, I couldn't drink this all to myself on a Saturday afternoon, I'd be drunk before tea time!" the woman giggled.

"...And that would be a bad thing?!" Emma laughed, pointing to a bottle of gin which had already taken a good bashing.

"Hahaha! I like your style! Nice to meet you, my name is Kali. I am a neighbour of Nicola." She put out her hand. Emma took her hand and shook it in hers.

"Nice to meet you, I am Emma. I work with, well, for Nicola." As she rolled her eyes with a laugh.

Kali raised her eyebrows towards Emma "Oh yeah, and how does that work out for you then?"

"It is great. Honestly!" Emma sarcastically replied.

"About as great as it is, to be her neighbour too, I bet?!" laughed Kali.

Although Emma was the one who was sitting alone, it seemed that Kali was the one who needed the company right now. As the drinks flowed, so did the conversation. The girls laughed and cried. It felt like they'd known each other forever.

"I actually recognise you. I saw you in the park one day with your perfect little family, you made me realise exactly what I wanted in life," Kali smiled at her, happy to be sharing this news. When in fact, all it done was upset Emma and remind her why she was here in the first place. *If only you knew,* she thought to herself and wondered how she was going to graciously change the subject. Just then, Kali shared how this past little while had been so hard on her, how she thought she was pregnant but it had turned out that her period was late. And that her long-term boyfriend had been so distant and she'd hardly seen him.

Emma was relieved. She gave Kali a cuddle and offered her best piece of advice, although with her current situation she didn't feel she was in any way, shape or qualified to give it: "What is meant for you, won't go by you. That's what my Grandad Fred used to always tell me, and I think it is true."

After everything that Kali had shared with Emma, without any intention of ever telling anyone other than her parents, Emma found that she was sharing everything with this girl she had only just met. She couldn't put her finger on it, but somehow, she felt as though she knew her well. It felt so natural to tell her, like they were already friends. Or maybe it was just the alcohol. But either way, Emma found herself telling Kali that her husband just picked up and left with her kids over a week ago. She found herself wiping away the tears as she explained how she woke up this morning expecting them home today, but they didn't turn up. So now, she is here at her bitch boss' BBQ on a Saturday afternoon because she had nothing better to do.

Emma omitted the part about coming to tell Nicola exactly what she thought of her. She'd save that for later. For now, she was just enjoying the company. Kali was such a fun-loving girl, tears aside, and Emma loved how she made this once-perceived horrific event a pleasurable and entertaining one.

"Tomorrow morning, I am going to get my kids. Whether or not Dan wants to come too, that is up to him. But I am not giving up on my kids. They are coming home with me." Emma felt her foot digging into the ground as she said this, literally making a stand for herself.

In that instant, Kali snatched Emma's phone, put in her phone number and called herself so that she would get Emma's number too. She gave Emma back her phone, then on her own phone went onto her socials to add her new friend. Set also set an alarm for the morning.

"Tomorrow at 11am, to give us time to sober up a little, I am going to pick you up and take you to get your kids. I promise." Kali gave her a big cuddle and a squeeze. "I promise" she repeated.

She ended the embrace and pulled up a picture on her phone, "This one is my wee Hugo!"

Then and there the planets aligned and Emma realised instantly who Kali was. She couldn't believe she hadn't pieced it together earlier; knowing that she was a neighbour of Nicola meant that she lived in this prestigious neighbourhood too; her favourite tipple was Whispering Angel, she wore designer clothes and accessories. And the fact that now, it was glaringly obvious at why she felt so familiar and close to her already. Emma was one of her followers. She already knew her through her social media. Although they lived in the same city, they couldn't have been further apart in their worlds.

Before Emma got the chance to even bring it up, Nicola Smythe came swanning over with a tray of shots for everyone! "What a small world" she sang, "I didn't know you two knew each other! Here, have a drink with me!"

The drinks flowed and the three women from three completely different circles found themselves enjoying each other's company. Maybe her boss wasn't so bad after all. Just then Nicola paused the music, stood up and thanked everyone for coming. She done quite the speech, and all that Emma could focus on was that "life isn't about what you have, it's who you share it with that counts."

Here she was, at a party in a neighbourhood she could only ever dream about living in, with two very successful women, who had just told her that they still don't have it all. Emma looked up to the sky and admired the stars and the moon. She found she was focused on one of the stars. It wasn't the brightest star in the sky by far, but it was sparkly and beautiful and shone in all of its glory. It didn't seem to bother about the other stars that shone brighter than it did, and it didn't compare its self to the moon which brightened up the whole night, or the sun that illuminated the whole world by day. It was perfect in its own right. This made Emma think, she didn't have to be the best or have nicer things to shine, her life was perfectly imperfect as it was. She knew now more than ever that her family was everything to her and she was going to get it back, come hell or high water.

But there was nothing she could do about it now. The drinks were flowing, the laughter was circulating in the air and despite it all, Emma ended up having a great night and a much needed good drink. In the process, she had made friends with people who didn't know her but listened to her and gave her advice as though they already knew and loved her. It was such an unexpectedly wholesome chat night and it was exactly what she needed.

Chapter 34

Kali

After a few weeks of Michael working late nights, Kali was just bumbling through her to-do lists. She felt distant from her boyfriend, she'd hardly seen him at all and he didn't even know half of what she'd been through recently. She hadn't even told him about the pregnancy tests. How could she, they'd barely spent any quality time together at all. And the little time they did have together, was spent discussing mundane things like bills, shopping and work schedules. She just couldn't find the right time.

The image that she was portraying on her social media was absolutely not the real life she had. She found herself bitter and full of resentment towards Michael. What was the point of this life they had built together when they couldn't even enjoy it or spend time with each other. She found herself just roaming about her empty house in between shooting content and answering her DMs from her followers. But, the whole time, all she could think about was the baby she never had. The family she didn't have. No one to share her life with her.

Truth be told, she didn't really know where she stood with him. When he was here, and she wasn't being snappy towards him, he was being as kind and affectionate as always. He'd kiss her on the head, wrap his arm around her on the rare times they cuddled up on the sofa together. But he just seemed a little off, a little different. He worked every hour he could get; he was hardly here. And when he was, he seemed distracted, distant some-what.

It had been a cold, wet and windy morning but by lunch time the Autumn sun had shone in all of its golden glory. She decided to make the most of it and walk with Hugo down to her mums and get herself a Pumpkin Spice latte on the way. It was a Saturday so Michael was working and she didn't fancy another day alone. Just as she was heading out of her front door the neighbour from across the road came running towards her.

"Hi, I was hoping I would catch you today!"

Kali just looked at her, waiting to see what was going to come next.

"I have chapped on your door a few times but no one was ever in."

Kali nodded her head, still waiting on the punchline.

"I am having a barbecue this afternoon and I would really appreciate it if you could come? I feel that we perhaps got off on the wrong foot, and I would love to make it up to you?"

"Oh, I am sorry, but I already have plans, I am about to go down to my mums," she replied, trying to sound disappointed.

"Bring her too if you like?! It's just my family, a few work colleagues and some neighbours coming.

Nothing too big. But I would really love it if you could come? It starts at 2pm. It would be lovely to see you."

"Thanks so much for the invite. I will see what I can do" promised Kali with a smile, knowing full well that she would not, indeed, see what she could do.

"It's Nicola, by the way."

"Nicola. I'm Kali"

"Kali, it's nice to meet you. Properly, this time."

"Nice to meet you. Enjoy your BBQ."

She made her way to the coffee shop, picked up her drink whilst paying for two, and walked to her parents' house. The air was definitely turning cooler, but the sun was warm and the air was fresh, just how she liked it. She, of course, never missed the opportunity, and snapped a pic of her coffee, her new leggings and Uggs, and Hugo in the background. #autumnwalks.

It was a fair walk and by the time she got there she was well over half way to her daily step goal. When she got to the house, she rang the bell but there was no answer. She reached for the handle but the door was locked. *Eugh, what am I going to do with my day now?* thought Kali.

She turned around and started the long walk back home. The rain threatened with dark, heavy clouds, but thankfully nothing came of it. She thought about her neighbour's barbecue, and how the weather wasn't really on her side for it. She wondered why on earth she'd plan to have one at this time of the year anyway, surely that's what summers were for.

By the time she reached home, 12000 steps later and nothing really on plan for the day, she heard the neighbours party in full swing. There was music, laughter, and the smell of sausages and burgers was wafting over the fence. She thought about it for a second, but instead turned the key in the lock and went inside.

5 minutes later, she was upstairs topping up her face of minimalist make up just enough to even out her skin tone, a little contour, blush and highlight to sculpt her face, a little eyeliner wing and half strips of eyelashes, and a little bit of nude lipstick. She told herself that she would just go for a little bit, to show face. It's not like she had anything else to do anyway.

She went into her wardrobe, pulled out a long sleeve stripy top, and tucked it into a pair of black mom jeans. She rolled up the bottoms to reveal her ankle and accessorised with a gold anklet, a pair of gold hoop earrings, and her gold Gucci belt. She finished her look with a pair of black baseball boots. She wanted to look like she'd made only a little effort. It's not like she was planning on staying long anyway.

She pulled a bottle of her favourite rose wine out of her wine fridge, took a deep breath and headed towards the neighbours.

She went through the gate and instantly regretted her decision. She didn't know anyone and couldn't see the host. She wandered around looking, just to show that she was here, but couldn't find her anywhere. Just as she was about to leave, she saw a face she recognised. It was the family-woman from the park. She was drawn to her again just as she was drawn to her that day in the park but this time, the woman was sitting alone and she looked like she could use some company. Kali headed over and picked up two wine glasses from the bar table on the way.

"May I join you?" Kali asked, holding an empty glass towards her.

"Yes, of course." She moved her coat out of the way to allow Kali to sit down.

She put the glasses on the table, pushing one towards the park-family woman and went to open the bottle, only just remembering that it was a cork bottle and not a screw cap. "Hang on, I will be back in a minute!"

A few minutes later and Kali returned from the hosts kitchen with a corkscrew in hand. "I hope she doesn't mind; I have just taken this from her cutlery drawer!" she giggled.

"Whispering Angel!" the woman said, "I have wanted to try this for ages, are you sure you don't mind?"

"Of course not, I couldn't drink this all to myself on a Saturday afternoon, I'd be drunk before tea time!"

The woman smiled "...and that would be a bad thing?!" she pointed to a bottle of gin which already seemed to have a few good measures out of it already.

"Hahaha! I like your style! Nice to meet you, my name is Kali. I am a neighbour of Nicola."

"Nice to meet you, I am Emma. I work with, well, for Nicola."

Kali noticed the subtle eye roll as Emma said so. Judging the good vibes she already felt from her, she felt safe to test the waters with a joke, but serious question all the same. "Oh yeah, and how does that work out for you then?"

"It is great. Honestly!" jeered Emma with more than a splash of sarcasm.

"About as great as it is, to be her neighbour too, I bet!" laughed Kali!

As the drinks and laughter flowed, the girls really enjoyed each other's company. Although they were just learning about each other, and there was close to a decade of an age gap between them, they just seemed to click and hit it off instantly.

With the liquid courage, Kali eventually psyched herself up to say that she recognised Emma from the park, and that was the moment she realised what was missing in her life. Her eyes started to well up as she told the story of the mistaken pregnancy, and how distant she and her boyfriend had become. She shared her life, how lucky she knew she was to have everything that she did, and her wee dog was the love of her life. But it just wasn't enough for her anymore. She needed more. Emma listened intently, nodding her head and letting Kali spill out everything that had been happening.

Emma gave Kali a cuddle and said "What is meant for you, won't go by you. That's what my Grandad Fred used to always tell me, and I think it is true."

Kali sniffed back her tears as she appreciated the intent behind Emma's words.

"Maybe now just isn't time for you yet, but you're still young and have plenty time for all of that," consoled Emma.

Kali nodded. She knew she was right.

"Maybe it's better that you and Michael have a chat about it all first, see if you are in the same boat or not before you decide to start a family. Trust me, it really is such a big, life-changing commitment and you don't want to be making that with just anyone."

The thought of Michael being described as "just anyone" made Kali feel awful. He wasn't just anyone. He was someone. Her someone. The one she wanted to do life with. Kali made a mental note and added "Speak to Michael re: future" to her to-do list for tomorrow, whether he wanted to have this conversation or not, it was something Kali needed to know one way or the other. *Surely, he couldn't be working another Sunday?* she thought.

"Although, I don't know who I am giving you that kind of advice anyway…" Emma looked down towards her jeans, twisting the wrapper of the wine bottle between her fingers. "I haven't even seen my husband or my kids. He left with them a week ago and still hasn't come back. I was expecting him today, and he didn't turn up. That's the only reason I am here at this barbecue, with a woman who doesn't even like me and has made my life a misery recently."

Emma shared what she had been through these last few months, and how all she wants is her family back. But instead, it seems like she has lost them. But she isn't giving up that easily, and tomorrow she is getting the bus back to her in-laws and she is fighting for her family. Taking back what is rightfully hers.

Kali drunkenly promised that no way was she getting the bus there again. She was going to take her instead; she would pick her up and drive her to get her family back at 11am sharp. The women swapped phone numbers, and while Kali had her phone out, she showed Emma a picture of wee Hugo from earlier.

Tipsy after sharing a bottle of wine, the two girls were well into the bottle of Pink Gin. Kali picked up the spirit to pour another drink for them both when she caught a look of shock on Emma's face. Before she even got the chance to ask what was up, Nicola Smythe came swanning over with a tray of shots for everyone! What a small world" she sang, "I didn't know you two knew each other! Here, have a drink with me!"

She placed the tray of shots on the table, and the three women picked up a glass of a creamy bubble gum pink drink and downed it in one.

"Thank you so much for coming, it means the world to me!" Nicola put her arms around Emma and Kali's necks simultaneously and placed a slobbery kiss on each of their cheeks.

The two of them looked at each other and then at Nicola, and the three of them burst into laughter!

Nicola pulled over a chair and sat with the two girls. "I know we haven't gotten off to the best start girls, both of you. And that was all my fault, I am so sorry."

"No, don't be daft" consoled Kali. "I don't even know you, but I am glad you invited me today" she smiled towards Emma, acknowledging that she was happy that the two of them had met.

"This is just the start of things to come, I promise to be a better neighbour in future" Nicola placed her hand on Kali's. Nicola then glanced towards Emma "And, a better boss" and put her other hand on

Emma's. "Things just got out of control for a little while there, but I am back now and feeling better than ever."

Nicola stood up, reached for the tray, and offered the girls "another?!"

"Why not!" called both Emma and Kali, already in sync with each other.

The three women picked up their shot glasses and downed them in one. "Ok, it's now or never!" sang Nicola, as she made her way over to the front of the house before she addressed everyone in a speech.

During the whole of Nicola's speech, Kali couldn't help but feel like the words were somehow some kind of future reflection of the life she might have herself.

Nicola was successful, her family were well-off and they had everything they could ever need. Or did they? Nicola and her husband spent their lives focusing on their careers. They brought up their children to focus on their academic and extra-curricular successes, but none of that was enough for any of them. When actually, all that they needed was themselves; their family; to be happy and cared for, by each other.

It took a breakdown for Nicola to see what was truly important: family. That was it. Nothing else mattered.

Her words echoed through her mind, and she could see her life reaching a cross-roads. She had to decide whether she wanted to focus on her career and risk the idea of family life. Or focus on family life, and risk possibly having that chance with Michael. If he was distant and not wanting to be with her, then having the conversation about their future could be the final push for him, and their relationship could be over.

The conversation with Emma came into her thoughts, *"…see if you are in the same boat or not before you decide to start a family. Trust me, it really is such a big, life-changing commitment and you don't want to be making that with just anyone."*

Kali knew there and then that a family was what she wanted, and as much as it pained her to think of it, she wanted that with or without Michael. She could feel her heart drop as she thought of a future without him. But the thought of not having kids was non-negotiable. Going through a short spell of a suspected pregnancy was enough to tell her all she needed to know. The conversation had to happen.

Chapter 35

Emma

Emma woke up with the birds in the morning. Despite getting home in the early hours of the morning, she woke up before 7 am with a sheer determination to get her family back. Although she had done it many times this week, she spent time going from room to room, admiring them for what they are and taking them all in. She was proud of what she had achieved this week. But the biggest challenge was yet to come, and the nerves were getting the better of her.

Emma walked to the local supermarket and picked up her shopping for the week. When she got home, she put on a big pot of soup and as it simmered, she put away the rest of the groceries and prepared for the week ahead. The kids would be back, and she wanted to enjoy every second with them that she could. At least with the soup on, that would do lunches for the next few days.

Just in case Kali had forgotten about giving her a lift with all of the alcohol they consumed last night; Emma had looked online at the bus timetable and planned her journey for any eventuality. Just then, her phone vibrated. Her heart skipped a beat hoping it was Dan. It was Kali, although she was disappointed it wasn't her husband, she was more than thankful for the text:

Hi, I am just about to get
ready. Are you all set?
Kali xxx

Although she knew she was getting her kids back today, this text message made it all suddenly feel very real. A wave of nausea washed over her. She sent a quick reply and checked the time. 15 minutes until pick up. Emma spent the time making sure everything was done and away. She gave herself a quick glance in the mirror to make sure she looked decent and poured herself a large glass of water and two precautionary paracetamols. Emma knew she had drunk a fair bit of alcohol last night, and she didn't want a banging head to impact the mission of her lifetime: get the family back.

Emma heard the horn beep as her new friend turned up outside. She stepped outside and locked the door, and almost laughed as she noticed that this wasn't just any car that she was getting picked up in. It was a massive, black, shiny Range Rover: the car of dreams. Or at least it used to be. But there was nothing in the world that Emma wanted more than to have her family back where they belonged; Together. Emma smiled to herself with her new found revelation as she hopped inside and felt the heated seats warm her bum.

"Kali, I can't thank you enough…honestly." A lump caught in Kali's throat and she turned to look away out of the window before she started to cry.

Before she knew it, Kali had her arms wrapped round her neck and pulling her into a much needed embrace. *God, it feels so long since I've had a proper cuddle.* Emma cuddled her back like she meant it.

She was so thankful to her friend for picking her up this morning. Whether she was getting the bus or going by car – it didn't really matter. She was getting back her family either way. But having a lift, and some company made it all that little bit easier.

Just as she had the night before, Kali filled the space between them with laughter and stories. Emma was so glad of it, it made her take her mind off of things for a little bit. But as they drew closer, the fear crept up inside Emma until it almost suffocated her. Just as she was about to open the door, she looked up and seen the girls dancing about in the living room. They looked as though they didn't even miss her one little bit.

The nausea returned with a vengeance and doubt filled her up entirely and all Emma could do was breathe it out.

"Good luck, you've got this. Go get your babies back! I'll be right here!" Emma almost got a fright as her friend encouraged her.

She suddenly remembered where she was and felt bad for her friend who had already gone out of her way for her. "No, just you go. I can't ask you to wait here. Just go, I can't thank you enough." Emma didn't want to waste any more of her time.

"No, honestly, I will take you all home. I am not bringing you all the way up here and just dumping you. I am here for you!" Kali rubbed Emma's arm, and it was just the reassurance that Emma needed to feel that it was ok to have her friend help her out.

"Ok, but only if you are sure. Honestly, the kids love getting the bus."

"I am not taking no for an answer, Emma! Now do what you came here to do!"

Emma blew out another deep breath as she realised that it was now or never. She looked up and gave a silent prayer to whoever was listening. She shut the car door and stormed up to her in-laws to claim what was rightfully hers.

Debbie answered the door welcomingly, and Emma stepped inside and walked into the living room. All of her fears and doubts of the kids not missing her were stamped right out like the embers of a fire. Luna and Fern ran straight to their mother as soon as they seen her and did not leave her side even for a second. Jasper's eyes welled up and he embraced his mum like he hadn't seen her for a year. She felt the tears nip her eyes as she saw just how young he actually still was. She closed her eyes in sheer happiness with her babies next to her, and as she opened her eyes, she saw Dan looking at her lovingly too.

"Come on kids, let's give your Mummy and Daddy some time alone," Debbie called to her grandchildren.

The girls clung tighter to her thighs and Jasper did not move.

"Go on kids, I am not going anywhere without you." She gave them each a gentle nudge. "I promise."

And with that, the children left the room reluctantly

with their grandparents and it was just Dan and Emma alone in the big, empty room.

"Dan, I love you and the kids more than anything else in this whole entire world. I have had much more thinking time that I ever wanted, but I done it for you." She took a minute and closed her eyes. "If you don't want me, then one day I might understand. But I need you to know now that I want my family back, and I won't be leaving today without them." Emma's eyes were still closed. She didn't know what his answer would be, and she dreaded it. She was awoken from her thoughts, with a big kiss on the lips and a tight embrace   from   her   husband.

"Emma, that's all I needed to hear. Of course I love you and I want you. We are nothing without you, and we have all been miserable without you holding us together. Mum has been great, sure. But she isn't you."

Emma was taken a-back by his reaction. This was not in her list of reactions or reasons at all. "What? Was this just some sort of strange test?" Emma could not hide the annoyance in her tone.

"Emma, no, you are getting me all wrong here. You and the kids are all I have ever wanted. But recently it's been like you haven't wanted us. The grass is always greener somewhere else for you. You wanted more than I could give you, but what you didn't realise was that I have given you everything that I could ever give you. Everything that anyone could ever want."

Emma looked down at the floor.

Dan waited on a response. But there was none. So he just continued explaining himself. "I just wanted you to recognise that. But you couldn't see it. We just weren't enough for you. So I done the only thing I could. I had to take it all away, and hope that you would realise that we were everything that you could ever need."

She processed everything he said, and he was right. As much as she hated to admit it to herself. It was such a cruel, and risky thing to do. But she knew deep down that if he hadn't, she wouldn't just magic this gratitude out of nowhere. It needed to come from within herself. No one else could show her what she had. She didn't realise what she had, until it was gone.

But one thing bothered Emma. "So why when I came before, you didn't take me back then?"

"Emma, you weren't ready for us. There was no fight in you. I said no, and you just accepted it. I thought we were going to come home with you that day as soon as I saw you. I was gutted. Truly gutted."

Emma nodded in understanding.

Dan embraced her and whispered in her ear "I am so glad you still want me, too. I was worried after what I've done, you'd never want to see me again."

"Oh, but I do want to see you again. Alone. At home. Very soon" Emma playfully nibbled at his ear as she did.

"RIGHT KIDS! IT'S TIME TO GO HOME! GET YOUR STUFF!" Dan shouted through to the room, desperate to get back to his home with his family, and to his wife, more than ever.

Emma laughed at the urgency in his response. He was still as cheekily-charming as ever!

The kids grabbed all of their stuff and kissed their grandparent's good-bye. Emma invited them around for dinner next weekend, as a way of saying thank you.

As they walked to the car, she went to say goodbye and thank you to Kali, but noticed she was drooling and catching flies instead! Emma tapped on the window and Kali jumped out of her skin, wiping the slavers from her face as she did so. Emma couldn't help but laugh at how cute and sweet her new friend was.

"Doze off there, did you?!" Emma giggled.

"Well, I was out with a couple of party animals, last night, you know?!"

"Oh, were you now? You can tell me all about that later" Dan pulled Emma in for a cheeky kiss.

"Kali thank you so much for bringing me today, but I am going to drive home with my family." Emma smiled as she said the sentence out aloud. Everything was finally perfect again.

"No problem at all, give me a call in a few days when you are all settled and we'll grab a coffee?" Kali asked.

"I'd like that very much" Emma was so thankful for her new found friend. She was a huge part of realising that she could have everything in the world, but it was nothing if she didn't have her family to share it with. With that thought, she almost leapt through the window and gave Kali the biggest cuddle. "I'll see you soon. Thanks again!"

Emma walked to her old, little car feeling like the richest woman in the world.

"Let's go home, family!"

Chapter 36

The alarm sounded in Kali's ear louder than ever. She got a fright, picked up her phone and checked the time - it was 10.30am. why on earth would she set an alarm for 10.30am on a Sunday?

She suddenly remembered. She was giving Emma a lift to fix her life and get her kids back! She rubbed her eyes and typed out a text to her new friend:

Hi, I am just about to get
ready. Are you all set?
Kali xxx

She put her phone on her bedside table, and rolled over to see that Michael was in bed next to her. She put her arm around his tummy and snuggled up to spoon him, nervously anticipating the chat that she needed to have with him later. He rolled over and kissed her the most welcome kiss. It's like they were teenagers again. Only now, they were adults who really hadn't spent any proper time together in ages. She melted into his embrace and couldn't help but smile the whole time they spent tangled up in each other. Maybe he did want a future with her after all.

Her phone vibrated with a new message:

*Ready to go. I feel
sick. Don't know if
it's the alcohol, or
the nerves. See you
soon. And thank you.
E xxx*

With only 15 minutes until she was due to pick Emma up, Kali jumped into the shower. A quick wash, throw on of comfy clothes, spritz of perfume and a freezing cold can of Diet Coke for the ride, and she was on her way to pick up Emma.

She didn't need the sat nav to guide her, she knew the area well. It was, after all, where she grew up. It was only about a 5 minute walk from her parent's house. She pulled up outside the semi and gave a quick beep. Emma came straight out, locked the door, and hopped into the car.

"Kali, I can't thank you enough…honestly" said Emma as she turned to look out the window. Kali reached for her and gave her a big cuddle, she didn't plan it, it was just a gut reaction. At first, she was worried Emma would not want nor appreciate any form of physical contact, but as quickly as the thought entered her head, it left her again as Emma retaliated with a tight squeeze as though she had needed that cuddle more than ever.

Kali slipped the car into gear and followed Emma's directions to her mother-in-law's house. At first the chat picked up from where they left off the night before. But as they drew closer to their destination, the chat slowed down until Emma was in silence, just nodding to Kali's stories. After a 20 minute journey, they had pulled up outside the house. Kali looked towards the house and seen the blonde and red haired girls from the park run past the large living room window.

Just then, she heard Emma blow out a long puff of air.

"Good luck, you've got this. Get your babies back! I'll be right here!" she said encouragingly.

"No, just you go. I can't ask you to wait here. Just go, I can't thank you enough." Ushered Emma.

"No, honestly, I will take you all home. I am not bringing you all the way up here and just dumping you. I am here for you!" Kali rubbed Emma's arm affectionately.

Emma blew another deep breath and looked left towards the sky. "Ok, but only if you are sure. But honestly, the kids love getting the bus."

"I am not taking no for an answer, Emma! Now do what you came here to do!"

Kali watched as Emma marched up the stairs and rang the doorbell. A friendly looking woman, Kali assumed it was her mother-in-law, cuddled her affectionately and let her in. When the door closed behind her, all she could do was wait.

She sat for about 5 minutes, looking to see if she could see any more movement in the house. But there were no more glimmers of blonde and red hair through the windows.

After a scroll through her DMs, Kali replied to as many of her followers as she could before she got bored. As she obliviously scrolled through her feed, she thought about the night before, about Nicola's speech, and specifically the importance of family and loved ones she talked about. And before she knew it, Kali was thinking about her own crossroads in her life. She couldn't deal with the thoughts, of that, not yet. She was here to help Emma. She would sort her own stuff out later. She clicked on Emma's page and scrolled through all of the pictures of her loving family. The home wasn't perfect, the clothes weren't perfect, the angles weren't perfect. There weren't even that many photos at all. But Kali couldn't see any of that, all she could see was the perfect smiles of the happy family; the way they looked at each other; the things they had done together; the experiences they had shared. Kali realised they didn't need any of the fancy stuff that she had, or that Nicola talked about. They had each other and it was enough.

Her eyes welled up at how proud she was of her new found friend, fighting to get her children back. Although Kali had barely even experienced a slither of motherhood, the fire that burned inside of her for it was intense. And if she was feeling as strongly as she was about having a baby that she wasn't even ever pregnant with, then goodness knows how intensely Emma felt about her own children. If these few pictures were anything to go by, it was a hell of a lot.

Kali put her head back on her headrest and closed her eyes just for a few minutes while she waited on Emma. Unsure of how much time had passed, she got the fright of her life when Emma knocked on the window, hand in hand with her husband on her right, her son on her left, and her two girls wrapped around each of her legs. Her face was red and puffy with delight.

Kali wiped the slavers from her cheek as she put down the electric window.

"Doze off there, did you?!" Emma giggled.

"Well, I was out with a couple of party animals, last night, you know?!"

"Oh, were you now? You can tell me all about that later" Dan pulled Emma in for a playful kiss.

"Kali thank you so much for bringing me today, but I am going to drive home with my family." Kali noticed the smile erupt on Emma's face as she said it, and witnessed the smirk remain there for a while.

"No problem at all, give me a call in a few days when you are all settled and we'll grab a coffee?" hoped Kali, eagerly anticipating the catch-up conversation with Emma.

"I'd like that very much" Emma almost leaped through the window and gave Kali the biggest cuddle. "I'll see you soon. Thanks again!"

Kali watched as the family of 5 piled into their wee car, jam packed full of people, and full of love. As they drove off, Kali wished to be as lucky as Emma was and one day have a little family of her own. She breathed out a puff of air and embraced herself for the journey to the conversation she was finally about to have with Michael.

By the time she reached their driveway she knew what she wanted to say, but she had no idea of how she wanted to say it. She didn't want to push Michael away, but she needed him to know that if he was going to be a part of her future, then there was going to be children involved. She decided she was going to tell him about the scare and she worried how he was going to take it. Would he run a mile? Would he be annoyed that she didn't tell him sooner? Would it make him realise whether he wanted kids or not? Just like it made her realise that she definitely did want kids. What if it done the opposite to him and made him realise that it was such a close call, and that he really didn't want any kids?

She couldn't put off the inevitable any longer. She turned off the ignition, stepped down from her car and locked her door shut. She barely even noticed herself walking up to her front door. As she touched the fob and pushed open the door there was a lit candle on the sideboard. *Strange.* She was confused. *I didn't light that. I didn't put that there. That isn't even one of my candles.*

Just then, she heard music coming from upstairs.

All of her worst fears came flooding to the forefront of her mind.

He's cheating on me!

The rage devoured her whole. Her eyes bulged and she felt sick as she considered her options: she didn't know whether to march up there and demand that he leaves the house right now with his little hussy, never to return again; to sit and wait for it to be over and let him find her sitting waiting; or to sneak up the stairs and catch them in the act.

As she processed each of her possibilities, her mind was made up with her final thought and she decided to sneak up the stairs, ever so silently.

She held her breath with each foot step, silently wishing she didn't find herself in this awful situation. The music grew louder with every step, as did her fury.

She put her hand carefully on the door handle to her bedroom and was ready to burst in on the potential about-to-be-crime-scene.

Chapter 37

Emma

It was a great day to be out with the kids in the park. It was much cooler, and they were all wrapped up in their winter jackets, hats, scarves and gloves. But that didn't stop Luna, Fern, Jasper and Julie's kids running around the park, and climbing up the frames and sliding down the slides.

Julie and Emma sat on the bench watching them play, catching up on the goss from the BBQ.

"Aw from the sounds of things, it sounded like a really great night. I am gutted I had to leave early," said Julie.

"It was so much fun, honestly you should have seen Nicola! She was such a hoot! She had us all on the shots and up on the karaoke and everything!" recalled Emma with a smile.

"That is hilarious! I didn't even know she had it in her!"

"Neither did I. But she is brilliant, honestly!"

"I never thought I'd hear the day that you would be praising Nicola Smythe, Emma!" jested Julie.

"If I am honest, neither did I, but over the last couple of weeks I've really gotten so much closer to her. I can't believe how wrong I was about her."

Emma filled Julie in on all of the songs they sang and the carry-on's that happened. She told the story of how one of the teachers was dancing on the table so much that it collapsed with her on top of it. They giggled thinking about how she will be feeling going back to work on Monday.

When the kids had enough of playing at the park, they decided to go for a walk to see if they could spot any wildlife and find any treasures.

"You know, I actually made a new friend too. Kali. The three of us have been speaking so much since the party. It's been really nice."

"As in athomewithkali? The influencer?"

"Well, yes. That's her. But she is so much more than that. She is the nicest!"

"Oh, is she? I have seen her about loads, and I follow her socials, of course. But I always thought she'd be quite stuck up and full of herself?!"

"God, no. Not at all!" Emma found herself feeling very protective of her new friend. "She is one of the kindest, most helpful souls I have ever met. I am actually having coffee with them tomorrow."

"Oh wow, coffee with the influencer and the head teacher! Check you out!" Julie curtsied towards Emma.

"Will you stop it!" she laughed. "They are just normal like us."

As Julie and Emma chatted, she found herself smiling at how things had changed so much. Not very long ago she was separated from her family and feeling so upset and lonely, not knowing what was going to happen. Now, she was on a little playdate and had friends playfully fighting over her, and her family were all back together and happier than ever. She watched as the children compared coloured leaves that they had found, and the treasures that they examined and popped into their pockets, with the biggest, grateful smile on her face.

"Mum, look at what we got!" shouted over Jasper! "I think we have about 251 conkers between us!"

Jasper, Luna and Fern each lifted the flaps of their jackets to reveal the shiny brown conkers that filled their pockets to the brim.

"We need to get these home, mum. They are so heavy!" Luna pretended to fall over with the weight of the conkers.

"Perfect timing, anyway, kids. Daddy will be home any minute!"

She could not wait to go home and see Dan. He would be finished work soon and she wanted to be there for him getting in.

"Thanks for a great afternoon, Julie" she gave her a cuddle. See you at work on Monday!

"See you then" and Julie curtsied again towards Emma.

The two of them parted ways in laughter and headed back home.

Just as the kids had finished getting their muddy shoes off and put them by the door to dry off, Dan burst through the door "Honey, I'm hooooome!"

Emma walked from the kitchen and embraced her husband with a big cuddle and kiss.

"Oh I missed you today!" she said, about to give him a kiss on the cheek but he turned his face so that she would kiss him on the lips instead. The intended peck on the cheek turned into a French kiss pretty quickly.

Jasper had caught sight of this and shouted "Eeeeewww! Mum and Dad are kissing!" just as 8 year old boys do.

Just then, the girls came running through to see their parents not kissing but cuddling instead. They wrapped their arms around their parents' legs and the 4 of them had a big group hug. Jasper refused to join, being too cool for that.

Bedtime couldn't come quick enough for Dan and Emma. The two of them had really realised what they were missing during the time they were apart, and they didn't want to ever experience anything like that ever again. They were so grateful to have each other, and they were obsessed with each other again, just as they were when they first started going out.

Chapter 38

Kali

As soon as she burst through the door, her emotions erupted into an eternal flow of tears at the sight she observed. Kali couldn't stop sobbing for a breath. Her whole world fell in on her, the room turned black and she dropped to the floor.

When she finally came round, Michael had his arms wrapped around her head, sitting on the floor with her. He was stroking her cheeks and kissing her. "Wake up, Kali. Wake up!"

He kissed her on the lips and she came round, trying to push herself to sit up.

"Woah, wait there a minute, Kali. You fainted. Give yourself a wee second."

As she processed what was happening, she looked to her right and seen that the room was filled with a thousand red rose petals, and loads of wee tealight candles spelling out the words MARRY ME. Only half of the candles were lit, the rest were patiently waiting, wondering if they would ever get to fulfil their life-long ultimate dream goal of being lit for the purpose of a proposal.

When Kali finally had the strength to sit up, she leaned forward and hugged Michael. He hugged her just as tightly back.

"This wasn't quite the way I had planned to do this…" Michael reached into his pocket and she closed her eyes tight in anticipation. She couldn't believe how much her life had flipped upside down in a matter of minutes. She opened her eyes and she heard an almost silent struggle as he finally pulled out a beautiful, shiny black polished box.

"Well, since I'm already down on the floor, technically on both knees… Kali Munro, I have loved you since the moment I met you. Always have, always will. Will you marry me?"

"YES!" Kali exclaimed, in utter disbelief. She could not have ever wished that today of all days, the day she had been dreading, could turn out as wonderful as it had. Not only had her friend reunited happily-ever-after with her family. But the future that she wanted, and feared wouldn't happen – a lifetime with Michael was confirmed. He did love her – he did want to be with her. The only final part of the conversation was whether or not he wanted kids.

She thought that it was now or never. She had to have this conversation now and establish their future together before anything else happened. If he didn't want kids, then as much as it would hurt her, she knew she had to find out now. Before anyone knew they planned to get married.

"Michael, I just have one thing I need to speak to you about first, before this goes any further?" Kali looked down, rubbing at her jumper sleeve as she asked.

"Of course, what is it? Are you ok?"

"I just need to know if you want kids?"

"Eh? Where has this come from? Of course, I do. I want nothing more than to have a family and grow old with you. That's what all this has been about." He pointed to the room he had beautifully set up. "I have been planning this for months, and working day and night to earn extra money for the engagement ring you deserve. I couldn't just take the money out of our savings; you'd notice it straight away!"

"Oh Michael, I honestly thought you didn't want me anymore. Or, that you were having an affair?!" she felt her cheeks blush.

"An affair?! You have got to be kidding, I can barely keep up with you, never mind having another! You are more than enough woman for me!"

"Michael, you gave me such a fright! I honestly thought you were up here with another woman, sneaking about and lighting her pretty candles while I was out!"

"I gave you a fright?! I burnt my bloody finger when you burst into the room!" as he suddenly remembered about the searing hot pain on his index finger and put it into his mouth for some relief.

Kali playfully slapped his arm. "You!"

"Speaking of which, will you do me the honour, and be my wife?"

"You already asked me, remember?!"

"I know, but the ring is still in the box…May I?!

She looked down at the most perfect engagement ring she had ever seen. It was a single stone, mounted on a plain shiny platinum thin band. The delicate band didn't look strong enough to hold the size of the diamond, but somehow it managed its job very well.

The stone sparkled in the candlelight and he lifted the ring out of the box and placed it onto her finger.

It fitted perfectly.

Michael stood up, put his hand out towards his fiancés and pulled her up and into his arms. He carried her onto the bed and may or may not have tried to conceive their first child that afternoon. And again before tea. And after tea. And during a film. And again before they finally went to bed – to sleep. And once more during the night. Kali had never felt so exhausted, but so alive, in all of her life.

Chapter 39

Kali

Kali was awoken abruptly by the sound of her alarm clock. She had it set early because she had plans to meet Emma and Nicola for brunch this morning. She went downstairs, had her usual mug of lemon and ginger and taken her supplements. There was to be no smoothie today, she wanted to keep room for the delicious food she planned to consume. It was getting a little bit too cold for her liking to do her yoga out in the garden, so she laid her mat in front of the bi-fold doors, so she could at least still see the sky, the grass and all of the plants.

After her workout, she went upstairs to take a shower when she noticed that Michael was still in his shower. She slipped off her robe and joined him. Now they were engaged and he had saved up enough to buy the rings, he wasn't working so much and they enjoyed every extra second of time together. But it was a Saturday and he still had work to go to. But she wanted the make the most of the little time they had together before he left. And she certainly made sure of that!

By the time she was getting ready, she really had worked up an appetite and her tummy started to grumble. She styled her hair and put on her perfected minimal make up look. She opted for leggings, a jumper and blazer combo. She finished her outfit off with a pair of sports socks, comfy trainers and a crossbody bag. The perfect comfortable but fashionable Saturday morning attire.

When she arrived at the restaurant, the girls were already there.

"Oh, I didn't realise I would be late, so sorry girls!" as she air kissed each of their cheeks.

"You're not late, you're actually 2 minutes early! I just got here early as I couldn't wait to see you both!" laughed Nicola.

"Dan and the kids dropped me off after swimming lessons, he's about to go for the food shop now," said Emma.

"Oh you dodged that one then!" chuckled Nicola.

"What a good egg you have there," said Kali, hinting for more, testing the water to see how things were between the two of them now. Almost a week had passed since she had taken Emma to get her family back. As much as she wondered and wanted to know how things were going, she didn't feel it was quite her place to ask. Emma would tell her when she was good and ready, she thought.

"Oh I know, he really is!" Emma gushed. "I never, ever thought I would say this. But I actually think that us separating for that week was one of the best things that has ever happened to us. Well, apart from meeting each other, getting married and having the kids, of course."

Nicola looked puzzled. "Oh my goodness, what's happened?"

"Ah Nicola, I wanted to say something but I couldn't figure out how best to say it. I wrote out a message so many times, but then thought it would be much better speaking about it in person. And just as I decided that you messaged asking if we wanted to go out for brunch and it was like it was fate!"

"Oh wow, I love when things like that happen" smiled Kali.

"So go on. What's happened?" encouraged Nicola.

"Well, it's a long, long, long story" explained Emma. "But basically, things had been a little bit rocky. Nothing really bad or that, I was just being horrible without even realising it. And I came home from the last day of term to a note saying he had taken the kids to his mums and that we both needed time to think."

"Oh my god, that's awful," declared Nicola.

"I know, it was just horrible. So I of course tried phoning him and messaging him but he wouldn't answer or return my calls. I was going out of my mind."

"No wonder, poor thing" comforted Kali with an arm rub.

"Hi ladies, can I get you something to drink?" interrupted the waiter.

"Can I have a latte, and a water please?" asked Emma. Her asking gave a signal of permission for the others to feel that they can order too.

"I'll have the same," replied Nicola.

"Me too" uttered Kali.

The waiter left to make the drinks with a promise to return in 5 minutes to take their orders.

"We better take a look at the menu before he comes back," supposed Emma.

"No, your story is much more important than our food" exclaimed Nicola.

"Trust me, it is a long story. Let's look at the menu first, we'll have plenty time for my story!"

"Thank God you said that! My stomach thinks my throat has been cut!" laughed Kali as she rubbed her grumbling tummy.

As promised, 5 minutes later the waiter arrived with their drinks, pen poised ready to write down their order.

"I'll have the avocado and bacon on toasted soda bread, please" announced Kali, keen to get her order in first.

"I'll have the smoked salmon and cream cheese bagel, please" requested Nicola.

"And I'll have the maple bacon pancakes, please" said Emma before she looked at the girls, "Dan always makes me and the kids pancakes on a Saturday morning" she smiled.

"So why aren't you having them with him then?" Kali asked sympathetically.

"Ah, we always have them before the kids swimming lessons. I did have a small one, but I was saving myself for now," she explained. "And I am starving for them!"

"Ok, so back to your story." Nicola was getting jokingly impatient.

"Yes, where was I? Yes, he wasn't replying to me at all so after a few days, I got the bus up to my in-laws. But he wasn't ready yet. So I just had to leave him, and my family there. It was honestly one of the worst things I have ever had to do in my life."

"Oh my god, so what did you do?" asked Nicola.

"Well, I went out of my mind. I kept thinking I was hearing them in the house. But it wasn't them. I just had to turn my energy into something positive. I spent time sorting out the house. I cleaned and decluttered everything. My wee mum and dad helped me do up the living room, too."

"And, you know how I said it was like fate that you text asking to meet for brunch?" reminded Emma. "Well, it was like that for me with you, that day up the hill at the view point too. Well, the same place, but a different time."

"Oh really, how?" chorused Nicola and Kali, with a swapped smile to each other.

"Well, I was out for another walk and I was sitting at the viewpoint thinking about everything. I had just decided that I was not taking no for an answer, and that I was going to get my family back in the morning. And that how I was really needing a good drink, and I remembered our conversation at that very point a few days earlier, and that's when I decided to come to the BBQ." Emma decided to leave out the bit about coming to tell her exactly what she thought of her, that wasn't something new friends done to each other.

"And, just as well you did go to the BBQ! If you didn't, the three of us probably wouldn't be here today," Kali put her hands on each of the girl's.

"Ok, so then what happened?" asked Nicola.

"That's where yours truly stepped in!" said Kali, settling into her seat with a little more pride. "I drove her to her in-laws the next day so that she could get them back!"

"Well, yes, essentially! That's what happened! Kali drove me to get my family back, and I left with them. I had never been so happy. And honestly, every day since. I just seem to be happier and happier as the days go on," smiled Emma.

"Really, in what ways?" asked Kali.

"Well, it's like we just can't get enough of each other just now!"

"Ooooh la la!" said Nicola, winking at Kali.

"Hahahaha! I know, but honestly, it just feels like we are in our early 20s again!" gushed Emma.

"I can relate to that too; the way James even looks at me now. It's just so good!" Nicola smiled to herself.

"Aw that's so good! It's just the best, eh?! And I don't know if it's because I sorted the house out or what, but I honestly feel like I love my home now. I was getting to the point where I couldn't bare it anymore. Everything just felt old and grubby. But now, it feels like a proper home... Actually, would you girls like to come round for a take away or something soon? Nothing fancy, just a night in our comfies? I would really love that!" asked Emma.

"I can't do the weekend, I have plans," said Nicola.

"What about Thursday? I do love a wee Thursday night event. It's like a little pre-weekender!" suggested Kali.

"Thursday would actually be perfect!" agreed Emma.

"I am in," approved Nicola.

And before she knew it, Emma had planned her first friends' event in her own home, and she felt proud enough of it to do so.

Just then, the waiter served the food, putting each plate down in front of the girls. Just as they began to tuck in, Emma shouted out suddenly that Kali got a fright.

"Erm, what is that on your finger, Miss Munro?!"

"Oh, this?!" Kali giggled. "I was wondering how long it would take you two to notice!"

Emma stood up in reaction and put her hands up to her mouth. "No way!"

"I can't believe you haven't told us this one!" Nicola questioned.

Emma sat back down in her seat, "I know, this is hardly something that has to wait!"

"Well, you hadn't said how you and Dan were getting on, so I didn't want to seem like I was rubbing it in your face or anything."

"Do not be silly! This is amazing news!" Emma leapt up and gave her a big squeeze. Then Nicola reached over the table to join in on the hug!

Emma pulled back from the embrace, her hands still firmly on Kali's arms. "Well, what happened? How did he do it?!"

"Well, the funny thing is. It was just after I got home from taking you Emma!"

"No way," Emma gasped!

"Honestly, I got home and there were lit candles and music on. I thought he was up there with someone else, so I sneaked up like a mad woman and there he was spelling out Marry Me with the tealights. Poor bugger burnt his finger and everything because I gave him such a fright!" Kali laughed.

The three girls were laughing at the thought of it all.

"So, when is the big day then?!" Nicola chipped in.

"Hold your horses, girls! I've got to announce it on my socials first. Don't get ahead of yourselves!"

"Oh, you young ones!" Nicola rolled her eyes. "In my day, there were no "socials" to announce on!"

"Well, it's changed times and I need to plan it. The reveal is almost as important as the event itself. And I don't want to miss any opportunities that may arise as a result of this" Kali tapped her head, nodding to her business brain.

"I cannot believe how different we all are," said Nicola, thinking out loud.

"I know…and look at us. A match made in heaven!"

Chapter 40

Nicola

The first week back to school was almost over. It was exhausting. Exhilarating, but exhausting. It was exactly what Nicola needed, just to jump right back into the deep end. The new way of working was implemented, and with only a few minor teething problems which is to be expected with a new project, things were going really well. The passion for her job was once again running through her veins. Just one more day and the first week would be done. But before it was over, she had plans with her friends to look forward to.

The morning after the BBQ a "Karaoke Kweens" group chat was set up and Nicola, Emma and Kali had kept in touch ever since. Nicola had seen more gifs, reels and memes in 2 weeks than she had seen in her whole life. *Oh, the joys of having younger friends*, she giggled to herself.

The three of them enjoyed evening walks together and the odd cup of coffee at the local café. But tonight, Emma had invited them round to hers, with the promise of comfy clothes and a take-away and Nicola just could not refuse. So, on her way home at 4pm – her new early finishing time on a Thursday, she swung by the supermarket to pick up a brand new pair of loungewear for her girls' night. She also grabbed a couple of bars of chocolate and some juice. Nicola hadn't been so excited for a Thursday night in a long time.

She picked up the kids and had their tea ready for coming home from afterschool club.

"Ok boys, I am just popping out for a couple of hours. I will be back before bedtime, so just make your way home from kickboxing and let yourselves in. I won't be too late. It is a school night after all!"

"Yes mum, we know," declared Jamie.

"You have already told us, Mum," said Nicholas, much more diplomatically than his younger brother.

"Ok, I have my phone with me, call me if you need anything" and she kissed each of them on the forehead, but just as she let go of Jamie, he clung onto her a little bit longer. She smiled to herself and closed her eyes, making the most of the rare hug. She looked down at him, ever so slightly, for 12 years old he was really tall already. "I love you, son."

"I love you, too." He looked back at her, his eyes slightly teary.

"I am fine, Jamie. Look at me!" Nicola spun around, arms out, like a toddler does when they learn they can make themselves dizzy for the first time. She knew he still felt guilty about what happened, but she promised herself she would spend as long as it took to prove to him that it was nothing to do with him, that it was her own mental health and that she was now doing better than ever.

Nicola went upstairs to get changed into her new loungewear and pulled on her trainers and gilet. As she walked down the stairs, she admired the picture that she asked James to put up in the entranceway before he went away back to work this week. It was the picture the 4 of them at the BBQ blown up and placed in the biggest, most beautiful frame she could find. She wanted it placed there so that she would see it whenever she left or entered the house, reminding her of the most important things in her life, her family. She smiled as she shouted to her boys, "Right kids, that's me away! Have fun tonight, and behave, I'll see you soon!"

"Oh mum, you are NOT going out in that are you?!" Jamie looked horrified at his mother's get-up.

"Oh Jamie, calm down! I am just going to my friend's house for a take-away. All the cool kids do it, these   days!"

Jamie shook his head teasingly towards his mum. "Ok, have fun then, "cool kid!"

Nicola left the house happy that she was well, she and James were more loved up than ever, her boys were safe and happy, and that they were a little more independent than they used to be.

A night in with the girls was exactly what she was needing.

18 Months Later

Emma, Kali and Nicola were all sitting at their usual table in their favourite restaurant. Kali had already tagged herself in the venue, and drinks were being brought to the table having already been paid for by a follower before they had even ordered.

"I'll have the steak cooked medium well, with the triple cooked chips and peppercorn sauce please. And a   coke."

"A coke?" accused Nicola. "No way. This is our monthly cocktail night. You know the rules! You better get that swapped for a cocktail right now!"

"I can't," Kali stood up and turned to the side, cupping her tummy.

"Aaaaaaah!!!!!! No way!!!" screeched Emma and Nicola in unison.

When they finally calmed down and stopped screaming, Kali passed out the cocktails that had been bought by her followers, "You two will need to share these between you!"

"Gladly" smiled Emma as she took a big swig of the daiquiri.

"You don't need to tell me twice!" Nicola winked.

"I can't believe it!" Emma was so excited. "I thought you guys were planning on going down the IVF route. I didn't realise it would happen so soon!"

"Well, that's the thing. You know we have had such terrible trouble carrying a baby."

"I know, honey" Nicola comforted Kali, rubbing her arm.

"Well, we went to our egg retrieval appointment, but it turned out they couldn't do it because I was already pregnant! That was about 5 months ago."

"But there is no way, we have been out so many times since then!" Nicola questioned.

"I know, it was so hard to hide it!" Kali laughed.

"How did you manage that though, there is no way?!" Nicola asked again.

"I just had to make sure you were both drunk and I ordered myself mocktails. I honestly thought you would catch on!"

Nicola thought about it for a minute. "Aaaah, but you've been so hungover. You can't deny that - I have seen you! You were sick in your garden bush just a couple of months ago, when you got out of your car!"

"Haha, yes I was actually!"

"Well, you can't fake that!" Nicola queried.

"No. I know I can't. I was sick. My morning sickness has been HORRENDOUS! But I have really enjoyed having it, in a strange way. At least I know constantly that I am still pregnant. We have never carried for more than 8 weeks before, and here I am 26 weeks."

"26 weeks? Wait a minute. You would have been pregnant at your wedding then?!"

"Yes, but of course, I didn't know that at the time."

"Oh no, now I feel bad for all of those shots we had. I had bought us a whole tray of them!" Nicola covered her mouth as she realised what she had done.

"Well, it wouldn't have been a celebration without Nicola and her tray of shots now, would it?!" laughed Emma.

"I do have to keep up tradition, you know! I do have a reputation to protect!" declared Nicola.

"I didn't have any of them, I just kept picking up one of your empty glasses and pretended to knock it back. You two had all of them between you!" laughed Kali.

"No wonder we were so drunk!" Nicola looked at Emma with a look of horror as she recollected just how drunk they were that night.

"Well, touch wood, everything is looking great! The baby is now viable, and although I am not fully in the clear, I am getting regular scans and check-ups. And I can't very well hide it any longer, my tummy is massive!"

"Eeeeeek!" Emma was practically squealing with delight. "And you are hardly massive! I have only noticed now you have pointed it out," replied Emma.

"I suppose it is lucky I live in big baggy comfy jumpers! Otherwise, you would have noticed a lot earlier" Kali giggled.

"It's so strange to think that I will one day soon have what you two have. I can't believe I am lucky enough for this to ever happen to me. I look up to you two so much. It is just a total dream come true. I can't wait to meet her!" Kali smiled down at her tummy, giving it a maternal rub.

"Her?!" Nicola didn't miss a beat.

"Yep," Kali smiled. "I am having a little mini-me!" Tears started to form in her eyes.

"You know," Emma declared "It is so bizarre to hear you saying that you have always wanted what I have. I have honestly spent years looking at your home, and homes just like yours, and dreamed that I could just have a slice of it. I wanted it so bad, that I actually nearly lost everything that was important to me. As much as I love my family, and I always have, I still just found that I was constantly comparing myself to everyone else and feeling that it just wasn't enough. Trust me, I know how important it is to appreciate what you have. I worry every day about my kids growing up and me missing things, or not realising the last time they do something really was the "last time." But I was just so focused on what I didn't have that I just didn't appreciate that they were all that really mattered to me." Emma felt her cheeks get red as she admitted the real reasons for almost losing her family, and how jealous she was of her friends.

"Oh Emma. I never knew that! How come you never said anything?" Kali asked.

"It's just not something I would ever say to a stranger. And then you became my friends, and you are both so much more to me than your house. And anyway, I know now that that's not what is important." Emma put her hands on her friends' hands. "I just looked online and seen all these amazing houses, and people living their perfect little lives. I would never have known that you had a cleaner to help, or how badly you wanted kids, or that you'd suffered several miscarriages. I had no idea about any of that. I just saw one tiny part of your life and compared my struggles to your highlights."

"Oh Emma, honestly. It isn't about trying to show only my good bits, I honestly just shared what I thought people wanted to see and what worked well for my business."

"No, and I totally get that now. It's just sometimes hard to see that from the outside, that is all. And the same with you, Nicola. I just looked at you and seen a scary, powerful woman. I was terrified of you!"

"No way! Haha, you have to be kidding. You didn't even know me!" Nicola acted insulted, putting her hand on her chest and opened her mouth in a state of faux shock.

"Honestly, I just thought you had it all and I wasn't even worthy enough to be in your company," admitted Emma.

"Emma! What are you like?! I am so sorry I ever made you feel that way. I just wanted the school to run well, and I don't think I went about it the best way back then. But I really do hope that I have made amends on that now, the school really is running so much better than it ever has," pleaded Nicola.

"Oh, and it really is, and I love it!"

"Have you decided to take me up on the offer of becoming a teacher yet, Emma? You know I would snap you up in an instant if you did!"

"To be honest, I have thought about it. But now is definitely not the right time for me, but maybe one day. Honestly, Dan and I have chatted so much about everything, and we found an analogy that sums it up perfectly. The grass isn't always greener on the other side…the grass is greenest where you water it."

"And never has a truer word been said" Nicola concurred. "I can 100% agree with that statement. "I tried single handedly to have it all, to do it all, to be it all. And all that happened was I had a mental breakdown, and then ended up being taken on by you two crazy cats! Oh the irony!"

"Hey!" Emma playfully punched her in the arm.

"Hahaha I am kidding! But seriously, it's true. If you don't water your grass and look after yourself and what is important to you, then life just comes apart at the seams. Literally!"

"Well, let's hope that the grass at our new house is greener than it is in our current one!" boasted Emma.

"A new house?!" asked Kali. "You kept that one quiet!"

"It was actually Michael that found it for us, and he got us a great deal!"

"No way, he didn't say anything! He's getting a little bit too good at keeping these secrets!" Kali looked down and readjusted her beautiful wedding and engagement rings.

"With Dan's big promotion we finally managed to pay off the debt we accrued. We have been saving up like crazy and have managed to squirrel away enough for a decent little deposit. It's not anything like the mansions you two have, but it is more than enough for what we need. I can't wait for you two to see it!" Emma could not wipe her big cheesy smile from her face.

"Emma, come on now, you know not to say that! It was you who came up with the whole comparison trap/sun moon and stars analogy," reminded Nicola in her best Head Teacher voice.

"I mean, it's not like she's ever stopped going on about it since," jested Kali, rolling her eyes back in her head pretending to be bored with the phrase already.

"The stars don't look any less beautiful, just because they are not the brightest thing in the sky, you know" the well-rehearsed words flowed out of Emma's mouth like a bird-song.

It was the first time that Kali and Nicola really and truly understood what Emma's saying meant. She had been wishing she had the lives that they did, all the while not realising how amazing her own already was.

Kali had the big house, fancy cars and almost a million followers but dreamed of having kids. After her loss, she longingly looked at families so much that she was willing to risk her relationship just to create one.

Nicola appeared to have it all on the surface, but actually she was barely holding it all together. She completely overlooked everything that was truly important, just to people please anyone and no one in particular.

The three girls drank their drinks and talked about how much better life was now that they appreciated what they had and how important it was to look after yourself and those around you.

"Cheers to not falling into the comparison trap!" Emma raised her glass and the three unlikely best friends clinked their drinks together.

"To not falling into the comparison trap! Cheers!"

Printed in Great Britain
by Amazon